Manage Yourself *to* Lead Others

Manage Yourself *to* Lead Others

WHY GREAT LEADERSHIP BEGINS WITH SELF-UNDERSTANDING

MARGARET ANDREWS

VENTURE
NEW YORK

Basic Venture
Hachette Book Group
1290 Avenue of the Americas, New York, NY 10104
www.basic-venture.com

Printed in the United States of America
First Edition: September 2025

Published by Basic Venture, an imprint of Hachette Book Group, Inc. The Basic Venture name and logo is a registered trademark of the Hachette Book Group.

The Hachette Speakers Bureau provides a wide range of authors for speaking events. To find out more, go to www.hachettespeakersbureau.com or email HachetteSpeakers@hbgusa.com.

Basic Venture books may be purchased in bulk for business, educational, or promotional use. For more information, please contact your local bookseller or the Hachette Book Group Special Markets Department at special.markets@hbgusa.com.

The publisher is not responsible for websites (or their content) that are not owned by the publisher.

Library of Congress Control Number: 2025934761

ISBNs: 9781541705685 (hardcover), 9781541705692 (ebook)

LSC-C

Printing 1, 2025

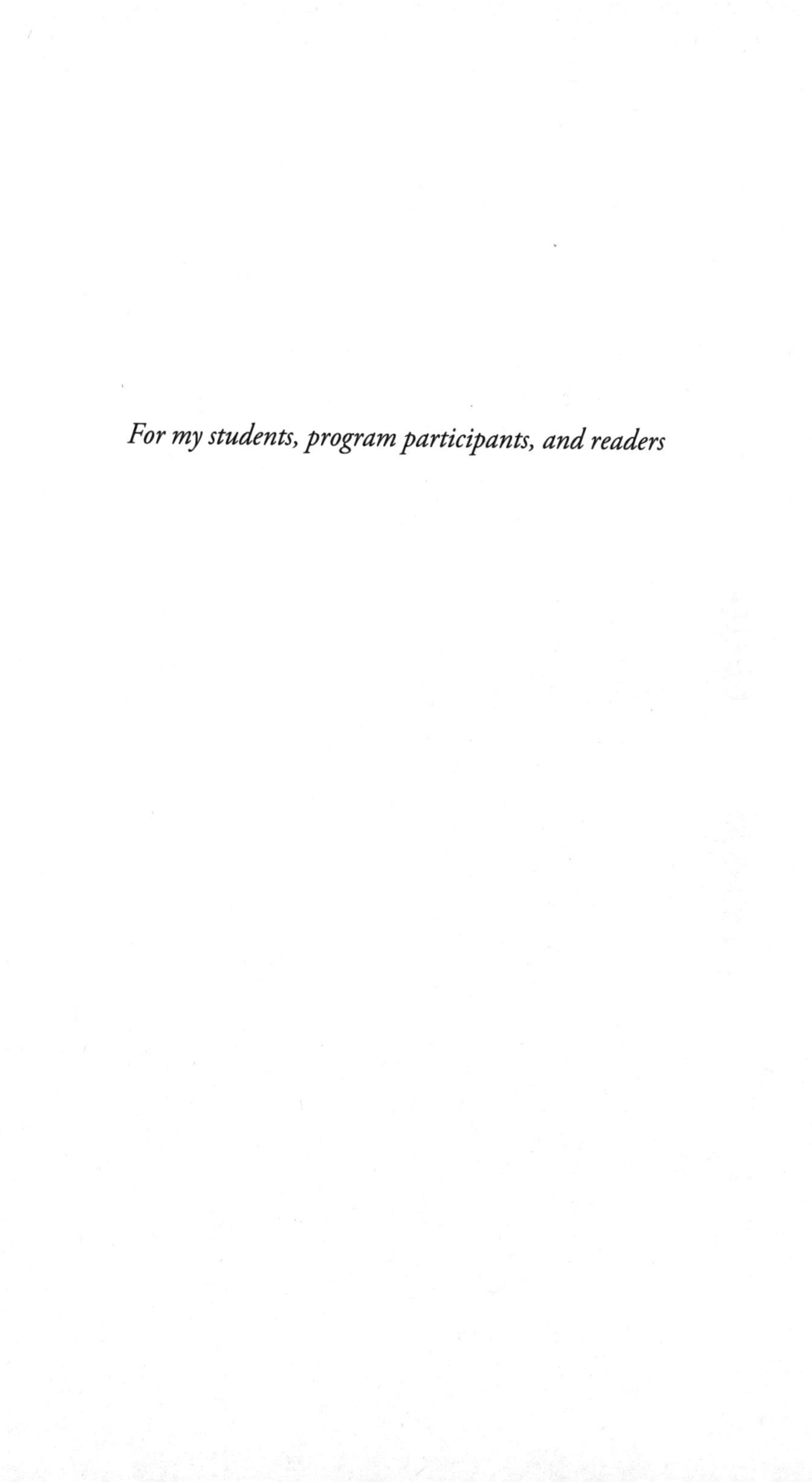

For my students, program participants, and readers

CONTENTS

INTRODUCTION

When Talent, Hard Work, and Good Intentions Aren't Enough

JAMES RAISED HIS HAND, THE first time he'd done so during the two-day executive program.

As his hand went up, we were nearing the end of a case discussion about Ron Ventura, a gifted neurosurgeon with *terrible* interpersonal skills. Taking the perspective of his boss, a hospital administrator, the discussion focused on what to do about this talented employee who performed his job flawlessly and whose talents had enhanced the reputation of the hospital and increased the number of patients seeking care there. However, this same surgeon was creating havoc in the operating theater and throughout the organization: barking orders, bullying and intimidating others, and generally running roughshod through the organization. During Dr. Ventura's short tenure in the organization, the hospital had reaped the benefit of his surgical skills in the form of increased revenues and profits. However, the hospital had also paid a price for the doctor's behaviors in the form of higher employee turnover, the fraying of a team-based culture, plummeting morale, and a potential lawsuit.

From the perspective of his boss, we in the class were discussing whether we should retain Dr. Ventura and try to coach him to preserve the benefits of his surgical skills and revenue-generating potential or terminate his employment because he was driving strong players out of the organization and creating a toxic work culture for those who remained. It was an intense discussion with impassioned and strong arguments on both sides of the discussion.

That's when I noticed James's raised hand.

"I'm Dr. Ventura," said James from the back row. Everyone in the room heard his comment and silently, in unison, turned toward his voice. He held the room. "Not the real Dr. Ventura, of course, because I'm not a vascular surgeon," he said with a half smile. "I'm an engineer, but the rest of the case might just as easily have been written about me. I'm a really good engineer, but like Dr. Ventura I've been an awful manager and teammate. In fact, that's why I'm here in this program—I need to learn to become a better leader. If I don't, I'm likely to be fired. Reading this case and listening to the discussion has been eye-opening because now I understand what my behaviors look like to others, and, honestly, I'm horrified by what that looks like. I was recently passed over for a promotion, and now I understand why."

In every class and executive program I've taught and every audience I've spoken to, there are people like James. Their backgrounds, successes, and setbacks are different, but many share a common theme. What has worked for them in their career is no longer working. Something isn't right. They've worked hard and had success, but currently they feel adrift. Restless. Stuck. Spinning their wheels. Sidelined. Passed over. Frustrated. These are the words that many people share with me in private, but James had the courage to express them out loud. They resonated with almost everyone in the room.

James's situation, although it may have felt unique to him, is fairly common among smart, ambitious, career-focused managers. We have energy, drive, and a strong work ethic that made us successful in our early careers. As we moved into higher levels of management, however, that work ethic, drive, and willingness to do "whatever it takes" to succeed suddenly weren't enough. The definition of doing great work has shifted dramatically because our work is increasingly done with and through other people. That's a different game with different rules, and not everyone gets a trophy.

Many business professionals, technical experts, and military, government, and not-for-profit leaders tell me that they are very good at what they do, but now that they're leading more people they feel out of their depth. It's a new way of working, and the stakes are significantly higher. Their education and training focused on the "hard skills" needed to excel in their work, and now that they're running the project, team, lab, unit, or company, they realize that they need a different set of skills. No longer can they rely on "just" their intelligence, drive, and good intentions. They know that they need leadership know-how. What they often don't realize is they also need something else.

We've Been Given Some Well-Meaning Advice That's Incomplete

When we find our wheels spinning, our old ways of working not working, it makes sense to learn more about leadership. However, much of what people seek to learn relates to best practices and tips on such topics as increasing productivity, managing time, running a meeting, negotiating a deal, setting priorities, or developing executive presence. These best practices and tips can be very helpful and may give us comfort in thinking there is a "right" way to lead, but they are incomplete because they don't go deep enough. A similar approach is to look for the "silver bullet," "the right way," or "the right answer." There isn't a silver bullet, a right way, or a single right answer.

There comes a point in our career where what we've done in the past is no longer working: Our intelligence, work ethic, and generosity of spirit are no longer enough, and the tips, tricks, and hacks we've learned can be helpful but not sufficient. We need a new approach.

Here's the truth: Talent, expertise, hard work, and good intentions are not enough. Powerful, compelling, sustainable leadership begins with understanding and managing ourselves. It's an inside-out proposition. Managing ourselves comes *before* leading others.

Leadership is ultimately about relationships, our relationship with ourselves and our relationship with those whom we lead. When we don't understand ourselves, we can't manage ourselves toward becoming the leader we want to become, the leader only we can be. That sounds like a waste of human potential. And when we don't understand ourselves, it's difficult to understand others, and this makes it more difficult to motivate them toward a common goal and develop them toward the leader only *they* can become. And that's a further waste of human potential. Powerful, effective leadership does the opposite—it unlocks and expands human potential in ourselves and others, and it begins with understanding ourselves.

Some people believe that spending time understanding ourselves is self-indulgent and self-serving or that leadership is about leading others and that's where we should put the focus. What they really want are the tips and tricks of leadership. However, understanding ourselves and evolving this self toward the person we want to become is the ultimate tip or trick in leadership. And it's not self-serving. It's kind—to ourselves and others. It helps us get closer to what we truly desire in our work and our lives. It helps us clarify our goals, become more grounded, settle into our power, forge connections, build strong teams, lead others toward a common goal, solve problems more holistically and creatively, and achieve better results.

It's the ultimate leadership superpower. These are simple, straightforward concepts that can be deceptively difficult to implement. It's not easy to develop self-knowledge, but it's the foundation of powerful, consistent leadership. Once we have this self-understanding, we can manage ourselves and begin to understand others better, and this results in the ability to lead more effectively.

People often approach me at a program break or after a speech to gain insight into their situation or circumstances. They're well-meaning, hardworking subject-matter experts, but something isn't clicking. They're not getting traction. They feel uninspired, restless, or stuck, and they think it's just them who feel this way. It's not. What might feel quite personal, and perhaps even shameful, is in fact quite common. Sometimes we think that "it's just me." It isn't.

I've Been There, Too

What James said resonated not only with others in the program but also with me because I've had my "James moment" as well. It came when my boss, Frank, uttered one short sentence: "You're not self-aware."

I sat in stunned silence as Frank went on to say that although he appreciated the incredible results I'd achieved, he didn't think much of my leadership style. In short, he told me that I was overly ambitious, demanding, and more focused on the work than the people doing the work and therefore didn't understand how my behaviors affected those around me.

At first, I downplayed what Frank said because it didn't make sense. I'd already had a successful career as a CPA, marketing executive, academic administrator, and strategy consultant. Before Frank's arrival, I'd had multiple, rapid promotions and had surpassed targets at each new level. I was among the youngest to ever hold the position and had received nothing but accolades for the work I'd done to date. Throughout all of this and across my entire career, no one had said anything even remotely like this before.

But the worst part was that Frank wasn't wrong.

It turns out that I had good strategic and operational skills but could be "rough around the edges," meaning some of my relationship skills were underperforming. I worked very long hours and could be intense and demanding, and sometimes I had difficulty understanding other people's perspectives. This could make my responses come across as insensitive and make some people on my team feel unappreciated and even anxious.

And my relationship with my boss was underperforming. Frank had taken over when my previous manager, who was one of the best people I've ever worked with, retired. It had been a rough transition from having a collegial, supportive, productive relationship with my previous boss to a strained relationship with Frank. I felt hemmed in, unheard, unappreciated, and second-guessed by Frank, and I responded by dismissing his oversight, minimizing my contact with him, and sometimes working around him. There was not much trust between us, only some strained goodwill. How much of this situation was because of Frank, and how much of this was because of my behaviors and actions? I'll never know, but I had contributed to the situation for sure.

Frank was right, though. I didn't understand myself or how my behaviors affected others, including Frank and several members of my team. It quickly became clear to me that if I didn't find a new way to lead, I was in danger of burning people out and undoing the incredible progress we'd made. And if I didn't find a new way to lead, I was in danger of derailing my career. These new revelations were hard for me to admit because none of this was ever my intention. But it *was* the result.

I wanted to change this result and began looking for insights from famous leaders, people I knew, management books, academic studies, history, philosophy, theology, and psychology. It was from this exploration that I found what I believe is a fundamental truth about powerful, compelling, sustainable leadership—that understanding and managing ourselves is the foundation of effective leadership.

This truth changed the way I approached leadership, and it made all the difference. Several years later, I created a graduate-level class based on these principles, and the class has had a waiting list every time it has been taught at Harvard for more than a decade. After the success of the class, I built an executive program centered on these principles, and it has become the most popular professional development program offered at Harvard. More recently, I wrote a keynote speech on these principles, and each time I deliver it, the speech resonates with executives across functional areas, industries, geographies, and organizational management levels. So I think that I'm onto something.

Becoming a More Effective Leader Is an Intentional Process

Few important goals are achieved overnight, and becoming a better, more effective leader is an important goal. It will improve your life and the lives of those around you. It might even make you a better, more grounded, happier person. It will allow you to take on bigger challenges and reach previously unattainable goals.

The Manage Yourself to Lead Others (MYLO) approach helps you connect with yourself to become more composed and intentional, which helps you understand and connect with others to lead more effectively. It's a layered approach to leadership development that starts with understanding and managing yourself, then moves on to leading others, understanding and managing organizational context, working through the inevitable challenges of leadership, and then setting the conditions and practices to lead for the long term. And it all begins with understanding and managing ourselves (see Figure 1).

This book will help you identify the leader you want to be and what you'll need to do to become that leader. The MYLO approach is relatively straightforward, but not easy. The process begins with asking yourself some tough questions and answering them honestly, and perhaps with more vulnerability than

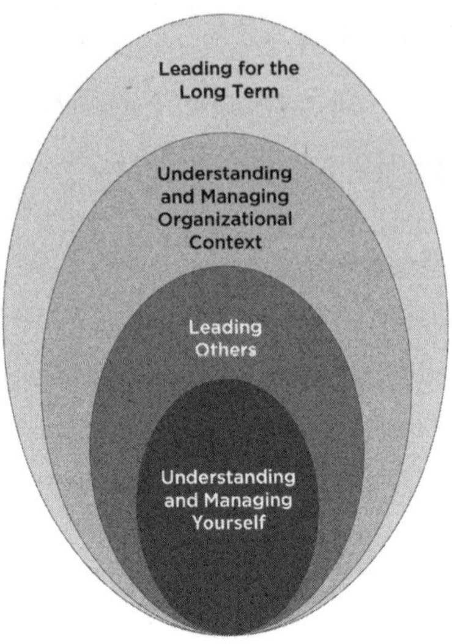

Figure 1. The Layers of Effective Leadership

you're accustomed to. These questions are about the people, ideas, and events that have influenced you; how you define success; what your real values are, the ones that drive your behavior; how well you understand your own emotions; how your behaviors affect other people; and, of course, how all these manifest in your leadership style, for better or for worse. You may be tempted to rush through these questions, but please don't, for you can make serious change only if you are serious about the process. For each of the exercises, I suggest how long to spend on an initial reflection. Returning to your initial reflections will give you additional insight.

You'll then use these insights to nudge yourself toward the leader you want to become through self-management.

Self-management is hard work that entails learning new behaviors, making many mistakes as you learn these new behaviors, dealing with some pesky emotions, being mindful when you're straying from your intended path, and stretching yourself beyond your current comfort zone to get to the next level of you.

We'll then turn to how to more effectively approach the problems and paradoxes of leadership, including "people problems" like leading and developing others and managing up, and how to understand and work through organizational culture. When it comes to effective leadership, there are no easy answers. Leadership is the human side of business, and because it involves humans, it can be complex, messy, and nuanced. As leaders, our job is to get results, and we have some choice in how we achieve these results. Although there are no easy answers here either, there are approaches and questions you can use to reframe problems; consider options, trade-offs, and consequences; and choose a course of action that fits the unique situation or circumstances.

Because you're likely the high-achieving, ambitious type, like so many of the people I see in my classes, executive programs, and speaking audiences, we'll also delve into what to do when you feel stuck, need to recover from a setback, or recognize that it's time to consider a new path. Sometimes things don't go according to plan. Projects fail, people let you down, plans don't work out the way you thought they would, and you may feel disappointed, marginalized, frustrated, or discouraged. Sometimes you need small tweaks to what you're doing, and sometimes you need to make big, bold choices to propel yourself forward in a new direction. We'll cover this, and here's a warning: There will be more questions for you to answer to gain insight into yourself and your situation before deciding, and embarking, on whatever next steps are needed.

I encourage you to read this book with a notebook and pen by your side, not only to answer the questions posed throughout the book but also to jot down your insights as you go through the chapters and read about the experiences and insights from other people who have grown as leaders using MYLO principles. It will also be helpful for you to revisit your initial responses and update them over time as you continue to grow in your leadership capacity.

Consider yourself a constant work in progress and this book—and your reflections—as the starting point for you to level up not just now but also in the future as you continually develop your leadership capabilities and deepen your impact.

James, who raised his hand during the case discussion I mentioned earlier, took the time he needed to work through the questions and exercises in the executive program and found out just how well the process works. Within a year of coming to the MYLO program, he was promoted. And within the next four years, he was promoted two more times.

The MYLO process works. It has been effective not only for James but also for many of the other managers with whom I've had the pleasure to work. These people hail from all regions of the world and include engineers and architects, police chiefs and project managers, hospital administrators and university leaders, finance directors and senior scientists, accountants and sales managers, lawyers and school directors, marketing managers and military leaders, and entrepreneurs and not-for-profit leaders. It can work for you too. By the end of this book, you will understand what it takes to be the leader you want to be, and if you do the exercises and answer the questions thoughtfully, you will have a road map for becoming that leader.

Imagine the leader you want to become. I invite you to become that leader by bringing the full power of your intelligence, ambition, and hard work—what got you here—to develop the next level of you. The leader you want to be. The leader you know that, with some level of vulnerability and stick-to-itiveness, you can become. The leader that, based on your unique combination of background, talents, and skills, *only you* can be.

PART ONE

UNDERSTANDING AND MANAGING YOURSELF

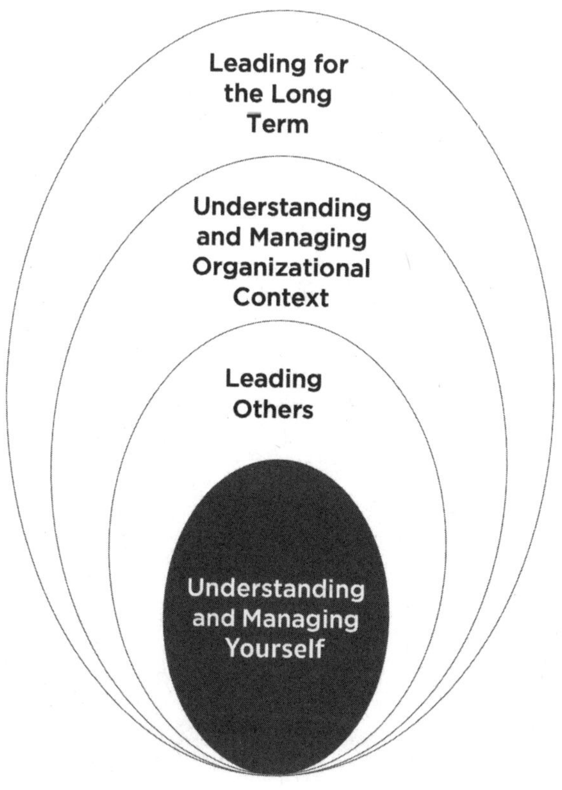

1

Recognizing What Great Leadership Looks Like

MOST OF US REMEMBER OUR best boss. Mine was Mike. A literary scholar, Mike had no formal training in managing people, but as he told me, "Novelists understand human nature, and leading is all about understanding people and what drives their behavior." I don't think Mike ever attended a leadership class in his life, but he was an outstanding leader and also the longest-serving leader in our organization's history.

I learned a lot from Mike. He never scheduled regular meetings, preferring to manage by walking around. He knew everyone's name, background, and likes and dislikes. He knew the names of your children and asked about them. He fostered collaboration, supported entrepreneurial ideas, gave everyone autonomy in how they did their work, and could change his mind when presented with a better argument. He praised in public and critiqued in private. He could also be paternal at times, and we didn't always agree with his decisions, but he made sure that we understood how and why he came to a decision. As a child, he escaped the full horror of the Holocaust because of the kindness of strangers, and this lesson stayed with him and influenced how he led. Mike took a long-term, developmental approach to people and gave everyone the benefit of the doubt, including second and third chances. He rarely gave up on someone, and treated everyone, regardless of title or place in the hierarchy, with great respect.

I learned a lot from working with Mike, including what it feels like to be both challenged and supported. I've had other very good bosses in my life, as well as several not-so-good ones, and have learned from all of them. What I learned from Mike is what great leadership looks like and, perhaps more importantly, what great leadership *feels* like.

In this chapter we'll look at what makes the difference between good leaders and great leaders, both from our own perspective and the collective wisdom of others.

Context Counts

This is a book about leadership, so it's worth asking, "What's the best way to lead?" Such a simple question, yet difficult to answer. For example, consider the following fifteen leaders: Corazon Aquino, Marcus Aurelius, Winston Churchill, Thomas Edison, Stephen Hawking, Martin Luther King Jr.,

Ernest Shackleton, Indira Gandhi, Katharine Graham, Frances Hesselbein, Abraham Lincoln, Nelson Mandela, J. Robert Oppenheimer, Madam C. J. Walker, and Jack Welch. What do these people have in common, other than that they are all considered leaders and were likely above average in intelligence? Not much, it turns out.

This relatively short list includes extraverts and introverts, those who came from wealth and those who didn't, those who sought leadership and power and those who stepped up to it reluctantly, some who might be described as "hard-nosed" and those who would be described as more empathetic, and some who had had experience with abuse, addiction, depression, disability, or discrimination. The list also includes those who applied their leadership to business and finance and those who applied their leadership to societal change, government service, or pushing the scientific frontier. There are many different leaders, with many different backgrounds, characteristics, and styles, demonstrating that there is no single right background, set of skills, or disposition that produces great leadership.

Each of the above individuals led very differently, and that's the point. Just as there is no single right background that produces great leadership, there is no one right way, or best way, to lead. Many different leadership styles can be effective, and the most effective leadership style will depend on the context. How we lead must be fit for purpose and must address the situation at hand.

The Best Person You've Ever Worked For

Let's do a brief exercise that will take less than five minutes and give you a better sense of what effective leadership looks and feels like.

Begin by thinking of the best manager you've ever worked for.

Before reading on, make sure that you have a person in mind and just one person. It might be the person you report to right now, the person right before that, the manager you had in your first job, or anyone else you've worked for during your career. Make sure that it's someone you know and have worked with, not a historical figure or someone famous you would *like* to work with or anyone else that you don't know. It should be someone you have worked *directly for*, not someone else in the organization you *wish* you had worked for.

Now that you have this one person in mind, think of the reasons they were (or are) the best person you've ever worked for. What is it about them that made you choose them over other people you've worked for? Write down all the reasons—the big ones and the small ones—why you chose this person over all the other people you've worked for. Try for a list of at least eight reasons.

I've run this exercise with thousands of people over the years and have heard many reasons that someone might be our Best Boss. It could be that your Best Boss was the smartest person you've ever known or worked with. It could be that they were the very best at some technical or functional skill that made them succeed at their job (e.g., programming, accounting, bench science, search-engine marketing, fundraising, risk assessment, technical writing, financial-statement analysis, carpentry, engineering, sales, surgery, etc.). It could be that they cared about you as an individual, challenged you, were good at listening, had a good sense of humor, pushed you to be better, supported your decisions, had vision, recognized unfulfilled potential in you, or nurtured your career. Or a host of other reasons. What are the reasons behind why you chose the person you did as *your* Best Boss? Before reading on, create a list of *all* the reasons—the traits, attributes, and behaviors behind why you chose this person as your Best Boss.

Now go back through that list and select the top three reasons. Exactly three. No more and no less. These are the three reasons that really made the difference in how they led and that caused you to choose them over other managers you've worked with. To get the most out of this exercise, please make sure to have your list of three reasons before reading on.

Now that you have your top three, let's look at these traits, attributes, and behaviors of your Best Boss. Answers for this exercise typically fall into three main categories:

- *Intelligence.* If you thought, "This is the smartest person I've ever worked with" or "This was the smartest person on the team," you're noting an intelligence attribute. How many of your top three reasons relate to this person's intelligence as being a factor in why you chose this person as your Best Boss?

- *Technical or functional skills.* Your Best Boss may have been very good, perhaps the best, at some of the "hard skills," those technical or functional skills that helped them succeed in their job. Whether it's auditing or animal husbandry, drafting or data science, policing or programming, research or retirement planning, marketing or machining, you may have chosen the person you did because you admired their technical or functional skills. How many of your top three reasons relate to this person's nonmanagement-related job skills?

- *Interpersonal skills.* These skills go by many names, including soft skills, relationship skills, smart skills, emotional intelligence, and even superpowers. These are the skills that are key to forming effective, sustainable relationships, the human-to-human skills that help us live and work with others. Answers in this category may be about how they cared about you, coached or mentored you, could build rapport with people, were open to new ideas, could find common ground between people in conflict, communicated well, gave you a lot of autonomy in how you did your work, were politically astute, or a host of other answers. Generally, if an answer doesn't belong in the intelligence or technical/functional ("hard") skills categories, it belongs in the interpersonal skills bucket. How many of your top three reasons relate to this person's interpersonal skills?

Do you have one of your traits and attributes in each of these categories, or is one category overrepresented in your responses? If you are like most people, the third category, interpersonal skills, is overrepresented.

I've run this exercise countless times in classes and programs across the world, and the answers are always weighted toward interpersonal skills rather than intelligence or hard skills. By a very large margin. This is true across countries, industries, functional areas, genders, leadership levels, and age groups. Although the weightings may change slightly in any given group, the overall trend is the same, with a cumulative average of 85 percent of reasons that someone is a Best Boss coming from the interpersonal skills category. The remaining 15 percent of answers are relatively evenly split between the intelligence and hard skills categories. Interpersonal skills are *always* the most important factor, by far, in every group I've ever worked with.

Other researchers have found similar results in what separates good managers from average managers, including a 1918 Carnegie Foundation study on engineers that found something similar—it was engineers' interpersonal skills that mattered more for success as an engineer than their technical knowledge. When they asked about the most important qualities for success as an engineer, they found that "personal qualities [were mentioned] seven times as frequently as [was] knowledge of engineering science and the technique of practice."[1] Among the most important qualities were integrity, tact, and "understanding of men," which also mirrors the Best Boss findings. The engineering study also notes that these skills "are usually a greater asset than technical knowledge and skills" to the person "who would deal successfully with human labor and skill." Daniel Goleman found something similar: "When I compared star performers with average ones in senior leadership positions, nearly 90 percent of the difference in their profiles was attributable to emotional intelligence factors, rather than cognitive ones."[2]

Intelligence helps us grasp difficult concepts more readily and leads to success in school with less effort than that needed by others. It's our intelligence that may have helped us do well in school and during our early career as we had to learn new skills and processes to become better at our job. It's the same with technical and functional skills. In whatever job we have, being good in these skills helps us to be good at our job. But they are not enough to make us a great manager. Once we begin managing other people, our interpersonal skills become much more important.

One time when I was running this exercise, one of the participants, Michelle, looked confused as she was thinking of the reasons for her choice of a person as her Best Boss. When I walked over to her, she looked up and said, "I'm realizing that my Best Boss wasn't actually the smartest person on the team." When I told her that to be a Best Boss they didn't need to be the smartest person on the team or even exceptionally intelligent, she wrestled with that idea for a moment. Later, at a break, Michelle couldn't wait to tell me about the epiphany she'd just had:

> I work in financial services, and this exercise completely changed my way of thinking about leadership. I've always worked with very smart people and thought this was the reason they were in those higher positions. My best boss was smart, yes, but not as smart as many other people I've worked with, but he was a *much* better manager than these others. But because I thought that intelligence was the biggest reason people became leaders, I've worked very hard to show people how smart I am and now realize I have it backward. I need to listen better, give people more autonomy in how they do their work, let people know that I care about them, the way my Best Boss cared about me and others on the team. *That's* the secret sauce.

Exactly.

It's not that intelligence or hard skills or knowledge is *unimportant*; it's just that for long-term success, it's our interpersonal skills that make the difference between a good manager and a great manager. Why? Because these are the skills that allowed your Best Boss to connect with you and to lead effectively. When I ask people if they would accept an offer to work with their Best Boss again, I always observe a sea of people nodding yes.

As we move up in our careers, going from individual contributor to team member to team leader to a leader of leaders, we move along a continuum from doing the work to leading others doing the work. Along this continuum, our hard skills become relatively less important while our interpersonal skills become more so. Whereas we needed our intelligence and hard skills to get us to where we are now, we need to develop our interpersonal skills to get us to where we want to go next in leadership.

The following comments about Best Bosses are from program participants and are indicative of what most of us value in a leader:

- "Showed care and demonstrated genuine interest in my life and professional goals"
- "Believed in me"
- "Cared about me as a person, not just an employee"
- "Challenged me with interesting work"
- "Exceptional listening skills—he really heard what I said"
- "Gave me a lot of autonomy"
- "Trusted me and gave me ownership"

- "Always made time to teach or answer questions"
- "Had a lot of empathy"
- "Valued my contributions and ideas"
- "Helped me grow and glow"
- "Made everyone on the team feel valued"
- "Made me feel like part of the group (I was the only female in an all-male office)"
- "More than a boss, she really supported my career"
- "Trusts me"

The most important traits and attributes mentioned from the thousands of people with whom I've conducted this exercise? That the manager *trusted* the employee, *listened* well, *cared* about the person as an individual, offered *support* and *empathy*, had strong *communication* skills, appropriately *challenged* the individual with stretch assignments and developmental feedback, and gave the person a lot of *autonomy* or *independence*. These are some of the most important interpersonal skills we find attractive in someone we work for. And they are all learnable behaviors.

These people aren't our Best Boss because they followed best practices—they *are* a best practice. They led, managed, and developed us *their* way and were able to get the best performance from us. The words and phrases you used tell us a lot about how your Best Boss made you feel. As poet and author Maya Angelou famously said, "I've learned that people will forget what you said, people will forget what you did, but people will never forget how you made them feel." Indeed. Our best managers, our Best Bosses, saw us and our potential, and they invested in us—and we remember them for this vote of confidence.

We Judge Ourselves by Our Intentions, and Others Judge Us by Our Behaviors

We chose our Best Boss because of the behaviors they exhibited toward us. It may be fair to say they had good intentions as well. But many people can have good intentions and behaviors that don't match these intentions. Some of our less-than-stellar bosses may also have had good intentions for being a good manager. But it was their behaviors we remember, and it's these behaviors we use to gauge whether they were a good boss or a not-so-good boss. If someone treats us poorly, it doesn't really matter to us that they didn't *mean* to micromanage us, ignore our ideas, communicate poorly, fail to develop us, show a lack of caring, make us feel small, or otherwise treat us badly. The fact is that they *did* do these things. Their behaviors belied their intention, and we judge them based on their behaviors.

As Stephen Covey wrote in his book *The Speed of Trust*, "We judge ourselves by our intentions and others by their behavior."[3] A corollary of this is also true: We judge ourselves by our intentions, and others judge us by our behaviors.

Understanding that we judge ourselves by our intentions while others judge us by our behaviors is often one of the biggest takeaways for people in MYLO. This understanding has certainly given me greater empathy for some of my not-so-good bosses. I now realize that some of their behaviors may not have matched their intentions. They may have had positive intent, and their lack of self-understanding or limited ability to manage their own behaviors got in the way. Perhaps our less-than-stellar managers did not "have it out for us" any more than we "had it out" for others we may have managed poorly earlier in our career. Just like us, our previous managers were still learning. As Harvard Business School professor Linda Hill says, "Learning to lead is a process of learning by doing. It can't be taught in a classroom. It's a craft primarily acquired through on-the-job experiences—especially adverse experiences in which the new manager, working beyond his current capabilities, proceeds by trial and error."[4] Just as we hope that others will forgive us for our leadership mistakes, it may make sense for us to forgive others while they learned to lead by making mistakes with us.

The Best Boss exercise also helps us realize that we already have a sense for what great leadership looks like and how these leaders make people feel, help people grow, and help people achieve results. The person you chose as your Best Boss, and the reasons why you chose this person, can give you important clues about what you value in a leader and how you might incorporate these insights into your own expression of leadership. What you value in their leadership style may be what you want to further develop in yourself.

The Leader You Want to Become

The leaders we most admire, whether our Best Boss or a famous business, nonprofit, military, political, community, or family leader, had to learn to lead. The same is true for all of us. Becoming a better, more effective leader is a process, a deliberate process, one that begins with understanding what type of leader, or person, we want to become.

Let's begin with three questions, looking at only one question at a time and taking the time to fully answer that question before starting another. To answer the three questions will take, on a first pass, approximately ten minutes. Revisiting the questions and your responses again later will give you additional insight. You can answer the questions here in the book, in your own notebook or journal, on a blank piece of paper, or by downloading a template from my website (www.margaretandrews.com/mylobookresources).

1. **What type of leader are you now?** What words and phrases describe how you see yourself and how you think others might describe you? Think about what makes you valuable as a team member and manager, as well as what may make you difficult to work with or for. These words and phrases may come from how you view yourself as a leader, from what you sense from other people's reactions to you, from language in current or previous performance reviews or 360-degree feedback instruments, and from discussions with your manager or teammates.

2. **What type of leader do you want to become?** What words and phrases describe the type of leader you want to become? Think about how you might like to describe yourself in the future and how you would want others to describe you. Envision how this new you would behave. For this question, it may be helpful to think of people you know and admire and the qualities, characteristics, behaviors, and actions of theirs you would like to develop in yourself. These can be your Best Boss or other current and former managers, teammates, and people who work with and for you. Please do not use public figures or fictional characters in thinking through your answers to this question: You do not have direct experience with them. Use people you know personally and have worked with. Try to be as specific as possible with your words (e.g., "calm in the midst of chaos," "empathetic listener," "as thoughtful and deliberate as Monique," "relationship builder and networker, like Rob," "creative problem solver like George," "caring and supportive of my team," "a trusted adviser," or "captivating, expressive speaker, like Kate") and not be too general (e.g., "a better leader").

3. **What is the difference between the leader you want to be and the one you are now?** In particular, what behaviors or skills will you need to develop or change to become the leader you want to be? This can include behaviors you want to start doing

more consistently (e.g., speaking up, listening more thoroughly, communicating with intent, taking calculated risks, being more open to others' ideas) or stop doing (e.g., micromanaging, interrupting, dismissing others' ideas, being defensive). Your list may also contain skills you would like to develop (e.g., making higher-quality decisions, becoming a more compelling speaker, putting people at ease). The more specific you can be in identifying the skills and behaviors, the more helpful it will be for developing into the leader you want to become. Choose skills or behaviors that will get you closer to the leader you want to become, remembering, as we learned earlier in this chapter, it is our behaviors as a leader, rather than our intelligence or technical or functional skills, that most affect others. So pay close attention to any behaviors you would like to develop or modify. Make a list and circle one to three of the most important skills or behaviors that will help you develop into the leader you would like to become. Now phrase these as "moving toward" goals rather than "moving away" goals (e.g., "Give people the time and space to complete their thoughts" rather than "Stop interrupting," or "Fully listen to others to understand what is behind their words" rather than "Stop making people feel small and unheard"). This type of framing will

> make it a bit easier to move toward what you want rather than away from what you don't want.[5]

Being clear about our goals for what we want to achieve for ourselves as a leader and as a human being is the first step in becoming that person. Understanding where we're starting from and where we want to go helps us understand our starting point and what mastery, or success, will look like. And specificity helps. Here are some examples:

Martin

1. *The leader I am now*: Results-oriented, competitive, hands-on, lose my cool/composure when angry; people have told me I can be charismatic, but also brash and intimidating
2. *The leader I want to become*: Better able to manage my emotions, particularly anger; more measured and deliberate in how I interact with others; coaching those on my team more than telling where they're wrong or what to do
3. *What will help me get there*: Focus on, and acknowledge, what emotions I'm having in the moment; harness the ability to manage my emotions when I'm in a stressful situation

Charlotte

1. *The leader I am now*: Achievement-oriented, detail-oriented, impatient when others don't understand my ideas or don't learn quickly, sometimes feel threatened and defensive when I am challenged or proven wrong, have received feedback that I always feel the need to be right or win an argument
2. *The leader I want to become*: More patient with others, focused as much on relationships as the tasks
3. *What will help me get there*: Take a long-term perspective when working with others (beyond just the project at hand) to focus on the relationship; being more open to different approaches and perspectives

Vivek

1. *The leader I am now*: Entrepreneurial, know what I want, always looking for a better way to do things, which can often come across to others that I'm criticizing them or their work; I've been told that I can come across as closed-minded to others' ideas and they often feel that "it's my way or the highway"
2. *The leader I want to become*: Someone who is able to get the best ideas from others and build consensus on the team for how to move forward
3. *What will help me get there*: Have discussions with people who see things differently and focus on what I can learn from them rather than trying to convince

them that my view is better; build on others' ideas; remember that I don't have to win every argument and that someone else may have a better idea

Irene

1. *The leader I am now*: Cautious, caring, don't always say what I mean and get frustrated when others don't figure out what I'm hinting at; have been told that people view me as a micromanager and that I need to be more clear in my expectations for people and outcomes
2. *The leader I want to become*: Direct, clear, and assertive in my communications, calculated risk-taker
3. *What will help me get there*: Take small risks to begin—like approaching people for a conversation, being assertive—saying what I want and what I mean while considering the other person's wants and needs; be clear about my expectations for others and let them figure out how to reach those expectations (without me telling them and watching over them); pay attention to how my behaviors make people feel

What are your answers to these three questions?

2

Understanding How We Grow as Leaders—and What Happens When We Don't

We had just finished a meeting with a client, and Bob, the senior partner on the project, and the early-career version of me were driving from the client site to the airport to fly home to Boston. "How do you think the meeting went?" he asked.

"Well," I said.

"How do you think you did in the meeting?" he responded.

For this question I didn't have an answer; I'd said very little throughout the meeting, other than introducing myself and saying goodbye. From the smile on Bob's face, it was clear he had an answer, and he was gentle and direct in delivering it: "That client is paying us a lot of money to help his company solve a difficult problem. One thing you should keep in mind is that in client meetings, the client will infer how much value you bring to the team and the project by what you say in meetings. In that meeting you didn't say anything."

Bob was right; I hadn't said anything of substance. As the youngest, least-experienced person in the room, I'd been intimidated by the industry-specific knowledge and experience everyone else in the room had and I lacked. I'd been nervous and self-conscious throughout, wanting to engage in the discussion yet keeping quiet out of fear of appearing as the inexperienced, uncertain newbie I felt like inside.

"I know you have good ideas about the analyses to run and potential solutions to the client's problems because you've shared many of these ideas with me," Bob continued. "But you didn't share them with the client, so now there may be a big question mark in his head about the value you bring to the project."

Now I felt embarrassed, as if I'd disappointed a partner and let down the firm, which is never a good feeling. But Bob wasn't finished: "I think you're an introvert?"

I nodded.

"I thought so," he continued, "which means you'll need to work a little harder at this. Here's my suggestion: For every future meeting you're in, before you walk into the meeting, think of three points you might make or three questions you have, and then launch into one of those points or questions very early in the meeting. It will get you into the game and prime your pump for more points and questions, and then you'll feel more comfortable speaking up throughout the meeting."

As an introvert, I was very good at observing and listening, and less comfortable about inserting myself into discussions. The awkwardness and fear I felt must have shown on my face, but Bob laughed and told me to give it a try. So I did.

Bob's advice was spot-on, but it took me many months to really get it right and feel comfortable doing so. In the beginning I focused on myself, and feeling self-conscious about contributing to the dialogue, I sometimes blurted out a question or comment too early and derailed the conversation, either stopping forward motion or taking it in a different direction. Other times, correcting for the earlier mistake, I would wait too long for the perfect moment and hear someone else ask "my" question or make "my" comment. Over time I got better at speaking up in meetings and was routinely, and confidently, contributing to the discussion. Beyond just speaking up, I became a more fully contributing member of the team and began connecting with clients. Bob's advice helped me prepare for meetings, thinking ahead about the big picture and relating it to the problem we were trying to solve, and how my questions and ideas could influence our work and give the client a better, more robust solution. But it was not a quick fix.

This chapter is about beginning to envision the leader you want to become, then identifying the steps it will take to get you there.

The Evolution of a Leader

We are always in the process of becoming. This was true when you were a baby learning to walk and talk, as a young athlete learning how to get better, as a student learning new subjects, as an entry-level employee learning what it takes to do your job, as you first began managing others and realizing it was harder than it looked, and today as an experienced leader improving your craft. Now that you understand the skills and behaviors you'll need to evolve to become the leader you'd like to be, it's time to begin the work. Whether it's speaking more (or less) in meetings, becoming a more skillful listener, being able to admit and learn from mistakes, delegating more effectively, or any other abilities you seek to develop, it will take desire, some thought, a plan, practice, and feedback to develop in these areas.

When learning a new skill or behavior, we're all beginners, and our results will show that we're not very good at this . . . yet. We often think that practice makes perfect and progress is somewhat linear, as shown in Figure 2.1.

However, progress in developing new abilities doesn't work this way. In the beginning, we're not good at all. Then, with practice and feedback, over time we get better slowly, then quickly, and then level off. Progress in learning new skills and behaviors looks more like the diagram in Figure 2.2.

Our progress follows a curve, an S curve, rather than a straight line. S curves, short for sigmoid curves, model the evolution of learning and development over time. In *The Empty*

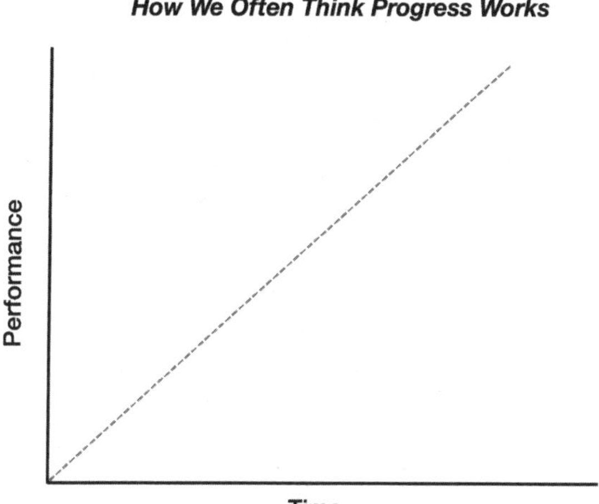

Figure 2.1. How We Often Think Progress Works

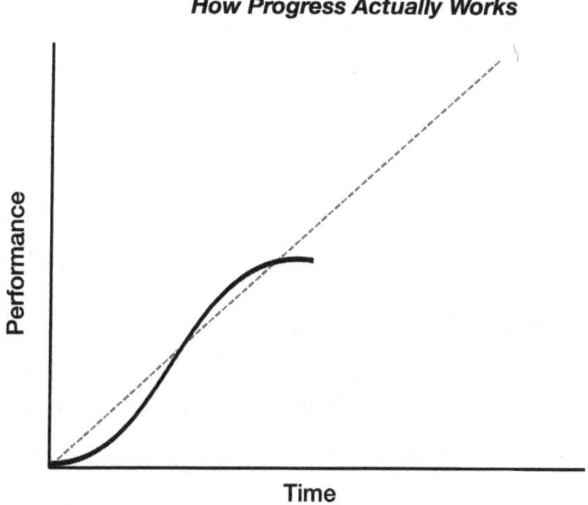

Figure 2.2. How Progress Actually Works

Raincoat, Charles Handy was among the first to see the relation of this mathematical function to individual and organizational development: "The Sigmoid Curve sums up the story of life itself. We start slowly, experimentally and falteringly, we wax, and then we wane."[1]

When learning a new skill or behavior, we get better slowly, then quickly. In the beginning we learn what's involved, look at others to see how it's done, think about what success might look like, attempt new behaviors and practice new skills, make mistakes, correct our mistakes, and try again with a more informed attempt. We continue this practice until we make progress, and as we do, things start to come together. Our practice becomes more effective, and we begin to get better more quickly, moving toward ease, comfort, and eventual mastery of this new way of doing things.

Once we reach proficiency and become more comfortable using this new ability, it becomes part of our portfolio of talents as well as a part of our evolving identity as a leader. It's now a skill or behavior we have mastered. It's now something we're good (or at least proficient) at doing. At this point, the S curve begins to level off, and additional effort on this new skill or behavior will bring only marginal, if any, improvement. To continue growing in our career, it's at this point that we need to develop additional abilities. This calls for a *new* S curve.

The problem is that when we launch a new S curve, we often get worse before we get better. When you look at the second (new) S curve (Figure 2.3), the performance level (shown on the

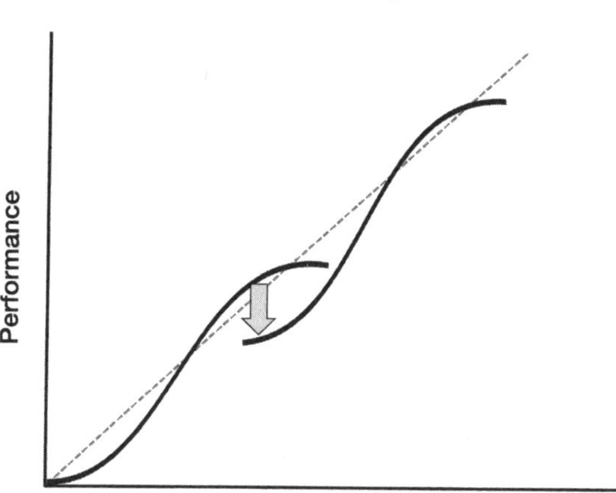

Figure 2.3. How Continued Progress Works

y-axis) is lower than the first S curve performance level. When learning something new, getting worse before we get better is to be expected. For example, we don't try a new sport and excel at it or pick up a new musical instrument and play a virtuoso performance, so developing new business- and relationship-related skills or behaviors will take time as well.

For high achievers, however, any drop in performance can be very uncomfortable. For successful, accomplished people, mistakes are something we typically try to avoid. It makes us feel awkward and vulnerable to not be good at something. We may need to pull from our reservoir of ambition and hard work to practice and be persistent as we make mistakes on our way to learning new skills and behaviors. As educator and executive coach Marshall Goldsmith says, "What got you here won't get you there."[2] Each new level of you will involve new skills and behaviors and will take time and deliberate practice, as well as making mistakes and getting feedback from others, to become proficient.

Trying on a new behavior, or really learning anything new, can make us feel unnatural or even inauthentic as we substitute a new way of behaving for an old way. Herminia Ibarra, professor of organizational behavior at London Business School, studies executive leadership and our wanting-to-get-better-yet-wanting-to-stay-within-our-comfort-zone impulses in learning new skills. Career advances require us to move well beyond our comfort zone, and learning a new ability can also make us self-conscious and unsure of our ability to perform at this higher level. Ibarra notes how, when attempting to develop new talents or change our behavior, we may feel as if we're play-acting or being inauthentic to our nature. Therefore, we "often retreat to familiar behaviors and styles." Ibarra advocates taking a more flexible, nuanced approach to thinking about our nature: "By viewing ourselves as works in progress and evolving our professional identities through trial and error, we can develop a personal style that feels right to us and suits our organizations' changing needs. This takes courage because learning, by definition, starts with unnatural and often superficial behaviors that can make us feel calculating instead of genuine and spontaneous . . . [, and] a too-rigid self-concept becomes an anchor that keeps us from sailing forth."[3]

The same thing happens to all of us as we advance in our career. Whatever new behavior we're attempting to learn feels unnatural for a while, and then we get better slowly, then quickly. And then it's time to master a new behavior. And then another. Early in our career, we have to learn many new skills and behaviors, including learning technical and functional skills, how to quickly understand a situation and think through options, ask insightful questions that get to the heart of the issue, and create compelling and convincing presentations. As our careers evolve, we master these skills and then have to expand our portfolio of abilities to suit the changes in our career and position. Instead of learning to speak up in meetings, we may have to learn to speak less and encourage others to speak up, and listen closely to what they say. We may also have to stop trying to do everything ourselves and learn to delegate effectively, as well as how to influence, build an effective team, and develop others. Later, as we move into larger, more public-facing roles, we may need to learn media relations, public speaking, crisis management, leading through uncertainty and large-scale change, and leading a team to think more creatively. Going from an individual contributor to a member of a team, to a team leader, to the head of a unit requires a significant level of development at each stage. There are a lot of S curves involved. Each new job, new promotion, and new level in our career requires a new and improved version of us. This was true for me, it's been true for my students and executive education participants, and the same is true for you.

You've been launching S curves your entire life and have been successful at evolving your portfolio of talents at each new stage. That's a good thing: There are many more S curves ahead, including ones ahead for the new skills and behaviors you identified in the Leader You Want to Become exercise in Chapter 1.

When you feel discouraged by not being as good at these new skills and behaviors, just remember that you've been maneuvering S curves for a very long time. Not only will you increase your leadership capacity, but your practice and your willingness to try new things and make mistakes in front of others as you learn will also serve as a role model for others around you, including coworkers and even family members.

What Happens When We Don't Evolve as Leaders

Not continuing to grow as a leader comes at a high cost—for everyone involved. On the individual level, we plateau in our abilities and limit our professional potential. Or we might derail our career. Just as a derailed train fails to reach its destination and can damage the train and the environment as it leaves the track, someone who derails in their career fails to reach their full potential and often leaves damage in their environment. Derailing in a career can include being deemed unpromotable by the organization; being sidelined, demoted, or forced out; or being given a reduced role, offered early retirement, or fired.

Researchers have found that people who had long-term success in their careers and those who derailed their careers had many similar qualities—they were intelligent, ambitious, made sacrifices for their careers, and had a good track record of success. However, those who succeeded through very high levels of leadership tended to maintain composure under stress, handled mistakes with poise and grace, and got along with a variety of individuals, among other factors. And those who derailed had poor working relations, had an inability to develop or adapt to change, and had difficulty leading teams.[4] Decades of research found consistent themes in why high achievers derail their careers, and some of the top reasons include the following:

- **Difficulty in building and maintaining interpersonal relationships**
    - Viewed as insensitive, abrasive, intimidating, or abusive
    - Comes across to others as cold, aloof, or arrogant
    - Poor emotional control; volatile and unpredictable under pressure
    - Blames others for problems
    - Frequent political missteps; alienates people
    - People avoid working with this person

- **Difficulty in building and leading a team**
    - Seen as authoritarian and autocratic
    - Micromanages; doesn't delegate or enable others

    - Inability to motivate and develop subordinates
    - Poor staffing decisions
    - Low staff morale; high turnover

- **Inability to develop or adapt/difficulty in making strategic transitions**
    - Difficulty in moving from area of expertise (i.e., technical/tactical level) to the broader focus at the general/strategic level
    - Overreliance on a boss, mentor, or sponsor for support
    - Inability to adapt to a boss with a different style

- **Engaging in inappropriate or immature behaviors**
    - Outbursts, overreacting, and losing composure
    - Inability to handle stress
    - Unwilling to accept responsibility for problems
    - Questionable integrity or sincerity
    - Gossiping and rumormongering
    - Inability (or unwillingness) to accept and act on feedback or learn from mistakes

- **Lacking strategic perspective/failing to meet objectives**
    - Overreliance on technical skills
    - Overwhelmed by business complexity

- Consumed with details and meetings
- Inability to prioritize[5]

The reasons for derailment hold true across industries and between men and women. As one research report found, "Derailment has to do with the fact that an individual is unable to 'fit' with the evolving demands of the job over time and at successively higher organizational levels."[6] In other words, what may have made us successful earlier in our career is no longer enough to sustain our success at progressive levels of leadership. Derailment is a self-development issue, or rather a lack of self-development issue. To continue to advance in our career and avoid derailment requires a commitment to evolving ourselves for the demands of the next level of leadership. Are any of the above reasons for derailment applicable to you?

Many of these factors in derailment relate to self-understanding—people don't understand themselves or how their behaviors affect others—or self-management, the desire or ability to manage our actions and behaviors. The point is that we can prevent career derailment and even bounce back from it by better understanding and managing ourselves.

Beyond the toll that career derailment takes on the person derailing, the above behaviors come at a high cost to the people they work with, the organizations they work for, and society at large. Unfortunately, we have an abundance of poor leadership.

Many of the above factors can lead to derailment, but they don't have to. As one report noted,

> Sometimes organizations have no illusions about whether interpersonal flaws are counterproductive but are willing to put up with such weaknesses as long as a person gets results and voluntary turnover is not a problem. Other organizations will put up with interpersonal flaws if a person has a spectacular strength (e.g., is a turnaround artist or a prolific generator of good ideas). One explanation for how these differences in derailment factors arise is that organizations have different cultures: different sets of expectations, beliefs, and behaviors which influence how people are treated, how one gets ahead, and how business mistakes are handled.[7]

We've all probably worked for people who had some or many of the above qualities and were tolerated in their organization or perhaps even promoted. It's also likely that we no longer work for these people or organizations because those who lead with these skill deficits typically have high turnover on their teams.

According to research, approximately half of all managers are somewhere along the continuum between ineffective and toxic, only about a third of employees are engaged at work, and direct managers account for more than 70 percent of this variance in employee engagement.[8] Despite the $366 billion spent globally each year on management development, in the United States only 14 percent of employees have confidence that their leaders can drive their organizations forward in the future. In addition, the leaders themselves aren't confident in their own abilities, with only about half of leaders believing they are well equipped to lead their organizations in the future.[9]

This leadership deficit comes with a very high cost to individuals, companies, and society in the form of anxiety, depression, unfulfilled human talent, high turnover, and an estimated $8.8 trillion lost because of low productivity.[10] It's a significant problem throughout the world, and it's something that we can fix.

I witnessed a high-profile career derailment many years ago when a senior executive at a Fortune 500 company was fired on the spot one day. This man, whom I'll call Paul, was a highly intelligent, successful, well-paid executive with a reputation for getting results. He also had a reputation for being aggressive, demeaning, and headstrong, as well as for being abrasive with the people who reported to him. One day, Paul's team went to his boss with an ultimatum: Either he fired Paul or the entire team would resign. The team won, and Paul was fired that afternoon. Because his behavior was known to many people within the firm and in the industry, he had few people he could call on to support him or help him find another job. It took him many months to find another job, and it was at a lower level and a much lower salary. It wasn't that Paul didn't have many good attributes—he was intelligent, hardworking, ambitious, and productive—but he also had some of the wrong stuff. It was his insensitivity to others and his difficulty in forming and maintaining relationships that ultimately derailed his career.

This is often the way that career derailment works—the worrisome behaviors were there all along and, at some point, outweighed all the positive aspects. Derailment often happens the same way that Ernest Hemingway, in *The Sun Also Rises,* describes how someone goes bankrupt: gradually, then suddenly.

Many of the above derailment factors have their roots in a lack of self-understanding and self-management. As we'll see in the next two chapters, most of us are not skilled in these areas, and this can make us difficult to work with and can hold us back. Even derail our career. However, when we understand ourselves at a deep level and manage ourselves accordingly, we can become the leader we want to be.

3

Understanding Yourself

PHIL, A DATA SCIENTIST FOR a California-based tech company, describes his leadership progression with one word: bumpy. As Phil told me,

> Several years ago, I took an executive-level position at a large media company and began leading people that led lots of other people. It eventually became a big team and a big job. I had my own office and assigned parking space, so everyone knew that I was on the executive team. With my new position, I thought I needed to act differently, more like an executive. Since my own boss had been promoted very rapidly in the organization and was the youngest person ever to be in his position, I looked to him as a role model and began to emulate

him. My boss let everyone know he was the smartest guy in the room, so I began to do that too. He made me feel smart and accomplished and did this by putting others down to elevate me, and I followed his lead on this as well.

My new behaviors made quite a splash, but not in the way I'd expected. At one point, I needed to let someone on my team go, and I didn't do it well. I'm somewhat conflict-averse and couldn't look her in the eye. She wasn't doing well, but I was immature in the way I handled the situation, and this left me feeling sorry for the way I had approached the interaction and very disappointed in myself. Right after this, another person on my team announced he was leaving, and the reason he gave shocked me—he said he was disgusted with me and couldn't work for someone who treated others so poorly. This really shook me, and at that point I had to look at myself in the mirror. I didn't like what I saw. Who would want to work on my team? I certainly wouldn't! Up to that point, I hadn't realized how much impact leaders have on their people and their emotions. I felt terrible, and that experience was my wake-up call.

Phil began reflecting on who and what had influenced him and the pivotal moments in his life and throughout his career, taking stock of these influences and how they showed up in his leadership style. At around the same time, he was in a leadership development program for Asian American leaders where the group was tasked with defining a leader in twenty words or less. The group coalesced around words like "strong," "decisive," and "inspiring" for the definition, but none of these words resonated with Phil.

He began to think about how he himself would describe a leader and found the word that most resonated with him: teacher. This is when, as Phil tells it, "I realized that, to me, a leader is a teacher who enables his or her followers to succeed and *helps* their teams succeed. This was a definition that excited me and one that aligned with my values. And looking back over my life, I'd been a teacher, mentor, and team builder in many situations, but had strayed from these behaviors because I thought I needed to be different as an executive." Once Phil knew his definition, he better understood the behaviors that would support being a leader defined as a teacher, rather than his previous approach of demonstrating that he was "the smartest guy in the room."

Phil credits his leadership turnaround to his stepping back, better understanding himself, and using that understanding to formulate a cohesive philosophy: "I became proactive about promoting the team, instead of bragging about myself." Phil smiled as he told me about the success of his teams, the awards that his team members have won in his company, how the people on his teams have gone on to bigger jobs, and how he remains in touch with people who have left the company. He went from someone who drove people away from his team to someone whose team people wanted to join. Phil's story demonstrates how we are influenced by the people and experiences in our lives, and how going deeper into ourselves, to truly understand ourselves as unique individuals, leads to greater success. It also shows how understanding ourselves and what type of leader we want to become helps us be intentional in how we present ourselves. It makes the behaviors needed to achieve our definition of a leader more obvious. And compelling.

What Is Self-Understanding, and Why Does It Matter?

Self-understanding is about clarity regarding who we are and what we want as well as understanding how our behaviors affect others. It includes understanding the people, events, and ideas that have shaped our perceptions, what motivates us, what we value, and what we want to accomplish in our time on Earth, both personally and professionally, and what we are willing to trade off to accomplish these things.

Self-understanding is the foundation of effective leadership. However, society doesn't emphasize self-understanding. With advertisers telling us what we should want and how we should measure success (usually money and the things money can buy), the power of influencers, the desire for "likes" on our social media posts, and often families that push us to "succeed," we're taught to chase what others have, to want what others want, and to care more about status and approval than self-understanding, personal growth, or living a meaningful life. Looking externally rather than internally leads to a lack of clarity about who we are and what we want, and this lack of clarity can lead us to make bad decisions.

The benefits of understanding ourselves well are immense for both our personal and professional lives. Organizational psychologist Tasha Eurich has found that "when we see ourselves clearly, we are more confident and more creative. We make sounder decisions, build stronger relationships, and communicate more effectively. We're less likely to lie, cheat, and steal. We are better workers who get more promotions. And we're more effective leaders with more satisfied employees and more profitable companies."[1] She also found that self-awareness encompasses both internal self-awareness, which involves how well we understand ourselves, how well we know what drives us, and how our behaviors affect others, and external self-awareness, which involves understanding how others perceive us.

Research suggests that many of us don't understand or manage ourselves well.[2] So how would you know if you're in this category? There are numerous signs, or tells, that someone is low on self-understanding and -management, including that they tend to be one or more of the following:

- Easily angered or "quick to spark"
- Easily offended, "thin-skinned," or taking themselves very seriously
- Poor listeners

- Concerned with proving themselves "right" or winning an argument, often at the expense of the relationship
- Highly opinionated or judgmental
- Limited in their emotional vocabulary
- Undisciplined, impulsive, and therefore unpredictable
- Unskilled at understanding someone else's perspective
- Defensive when receiving feedback
- Lacking in awareness about how their behaviors may be contributing to a difficult situation
- Unwilling to take responsibility for their actions, often blaming others for situations and outcomes[3]

In addition, many people who lack self-understanding feel misunderstood by others; this is because they don't understand that their behaviors may not align with their intentions and therefore how they come across to others. Many people who lack self-understanding are viewed by others as untrustworthy, which relates to them being unpredictable, impulsive, poor listeners who are unable to understand other people's perspectives and can't see how their actions and behaviors are experienced by others. This, of course, can be a leadership problem.

There's a high price to be paid for this lack of self-understanding. Korn Ferry research has found that leaders who lack critical aspects of self-understanding are 6.2 times more likely to derail in their career.[4] That's a large penalty for not understanding ourselves.

The importance of self-understanding is also not a new concept. "Know thyself" was carved into the stones near the Temple of Apollo at Delphi back in the seventh century BCE, and ancient Greek philosopher Aristotle taught that "knowing yourself is the beginning of all wisdom." Self-understanding not only is the foundation for leadership but also helps us be better human beings.

Even with the obvious drawbacks of having a lack of self-awareness, better understanding ourselves can be difficult to do because it's often emotional work. Some people are uncomfortable with self-reflection, thinking it may stir up memories and emotions from the past. Many people fear being vulnerable while they are acknowledging past hurts, mistakes, or transgressions. Others are unsure how to approach it. And some may think focusing on self-understanding sounds egotistical, self-absorbed, a bit "woo-woo," useless, or even selfish. In fact, it's none of the above. Rather than being self-absorbed or selfish, it's a form of kindness. It's kind to ourselves to understand what drives us and therefore how to put ourselves in positions where we will thrive because they fit with our strengths, interests, and values. It's also kind to others we live and work with, for self-understanding helps us show up more consistently, comfortably, and genuinely, which helps build trust and long-term, productive relationships.

Leadership emerges from our life story and our unique portfolio of experiences, influences, ways of thinking, values, and ambitions. Once we know who we are, we have our foundation. From there, we can envision the next level of ourselves as a leader and as a person, and determine what behaviors and skills we need to develop to become that person. And then the work of changing our approach and behaviors begins, which is real work. Hard work. But it all begins with the insight gained from understanding ourselves.

Six Questions for Self-Understanding

This section will take some time to process, and it's very important to do the work. Skipping over these questions or giving only a cursory answer to any of them may prevent you from gaining the insights into yourself that are important for becoming the leader you want to be. Managing ourselves comes before leading others, and we can't manage what we don't understand, particularly if what we don't understand is ourselves.

Please allow a minimum of thirty minutes for your first pass at this activity. Spend five to ten minutes per question, quickly writing your thoughts on each question without stopping to think too much, and definitely without editing your answers to what you think they "should be." Simply write whatever comes into your head, without judgment. Your writing may stir up some emotions; that's not only fine but also normal. After you've done a first pass at the questions, return to the exercise several hours later, or the next day, to review your answers, think more about the questions, and expand and deepen the answers to each question. Be as honest with yourself as possible. The answers and the insights they will unlock are for you and no one else. So go on: Tell on yourself and feel whatever emotions that may come up. The more thought and effort you spend in answering these questions, the more you will get out of this exercise, this book, and your own leadership potential.

Some people go through the questions quickly and at a high level, something I actively discourage. Short, cursory responses to the questions aren't enough to get much insight. In my professional development programs, after beginning to answer the questions while we're in the session, I ask everyone to go back and revisit their answers that evening or early the next morning in order to mine for further insights. When we meet again the next morning, it's obvious who spent time wrestling with the questions and pulling out the insights, and who didn't. It's the people who do the hard work of answering these questions honestly and fully who get the most out of the program and who begin to shift how they approach understanding and leading others. For many people, it can be an emotional journey as they more fully discover how the people and events in their lives have shaped their perspective and influenced them as individuals and as leaders. Some are surprised to see how they have been living someone else's values or following a set of "shoulds" that have little resonance with their definition of success. And others find they are living in alignment with their values or perhaps need only a few small adjustments to get in alignment.

It takes time and effort to delve into questions like these, put the pieces together, and pull out the insights. Not all of us feel comfortable with this because there is an emotional component to this exercise. As Phil told me, "Engineers are good at analyzing the outside world, not the inside world." It also takes courage because it can be embarrassing, and even painful at times, to shine a light inside ourselves and comprehend what we see. And Rohan Rajiv, author of the successful blog *A Learning a Day*, told me, "You get power when you own your story and lead from wholeness. Sometimes you have to dig into the unsavory parts to get closure." This may mean making peace with our past and understanding that what shaped us doesn't need to define us or, as C. S. Lewis so beautifully wrote, "You can't go back and change the beginning, but you can start where you are and change the ending."

These six questions won't give you "the answer," but answering the questions fully and honestly can help you array the information in such a way that you can pull out important insights to better understand yourself.

You can answer the questions here in the book, in your own journal, on a blank piece of paper, or on a template that you can download from my website (www.margaretandrews.com/mylobookresources). Please note that the first question is a *big question*. Of all the questions, the first one is the deepest and is likely to take you the longest to answer. It sets a foundation for the other five questions, so the time you spend answering the first question will not only give you insight into yourself and how you lead but also help you answer several other questions.

1. **Who, and whose thinking, has shaped you as an individual?** This includes parents, siblings, extended family, friends, lovers, enemies, teachers, coworkers, and even strangers. It includes people who helped you and people who hurt you. It can also include ideas from history, philosophy, religion, your community, favorite childhood stories, books you've read, classes you've taken, movies you've watched, talks you've heard, and conversations you've had. How have these people and ideas influenced your life and the way you lead?

2. **What situations and events have helped shape your perspective?** Think about situations and events from your childhood, college days, early career, family life, travel, and lucky (and unlucky) accidents. How have these situations and events influenced your life and the way you lead?

3. **What does success look like for you?** How would you define success for your professional life? For your personal life? Are any parts of your definitions of success related to some longer, larger sense of purpose? How have these definitions of success influenced your life and the way you lead?

4. **What are your core values, and how have these values changed throughout your life?** To help

you with this question, which many people struggle to answer, there are two approaches that might help. The first is to look at your calendar and see what someone looking at your schedule might infer about your values. For example, what takes priority over other things? The second approach is to think of things that make you angry—often things that make us angry relate to a value that's been violated or stepped on. Where did these values come from (e.g., parents, religion, schooling, friends, society)? How have your values changed over your lifetime, and what led to these changes? To what extent are you living your values and not someone else's? How do these values show up in your personal life? In your professional life?

5. **To what extent are you aware of—and allow yourself to feel—your emotions?** Part of understanding ourselves is being aware of our internal world of emotions and how they can often drive our behaviors. Are you aware of the feeling of anger? How do you behave when you're angry? How about when you are happy, joyful, sad, jealous, disappointed, fearful, or any of the other emotions we all feel? How do people around you respond to you when you're in any of these states? How have your behaviors when you are feeling these different emotions played out throughout your

life? How have these situations influenced your life and the way you lead?

6. **What feedback have you received over the years about how your actions and behaviors affect others?** This includes feedback you've received on a professional level, as well as a personal level, and both positive and negative feedback. Whether you agree with the feedback or disagree with it, the feedback you receive relates to others' perceptions of your behaviors and is a good indication of the impact you have on others. It gives you a sense for other people's sense of your strengths and weaknesses, and may sometimes illuminate a blind spot. At a minimum, their feedback is the gift of a perspective or point of view that you may not have previously known. What was the best feedback you've ever received? The most painful? The most surprising (either a positive or negative surprise)? Are there themes in the feedback? Are there patterns that relate to your self-understanding and self-management? Is the feedback relatively stable over time, or has it changed during your career? Does any of this feedback perhaps relate to not being aware of your emotions (e.g., anger) and how your behaviors affect others? What insights can you take from any of this feedback about how your behaviors are seen by others?

When looking at your responses to the Six Questions for Self-Understanding, what conclusions can you draw about how your past has informed your thinking? Your actions and behaviors? Your current situation? About what you value? About how you are following or living *your* values and not someone else's? About how you want to contribute to the world? What patterns do you see? Which ideas and perspectives still serve you, and which of them may need to be updated or rewritten?

Insights

Through the years I've had many people share their stories with me about how they've had important insights from these and other self-reflective exercises, and I will share four of them with you.

Katie Doran, a former MYLO student and now senior director of physical operations at LightForce, told me about an epiphany she had during class that changed her approach to work and leadership: "We had to figure out how to build something as a team, and I was pretty sure I knew the best way to approach it. I kept thinking, 'I am right' and acted out of confidence in this assessment. We ended up with the least successful output, and we had a terrible time as a team." During the feedback session after the exercise, Katie's team told her that she was a "bulldozer" and that her behaviors during the exercise caused the team to come in last place. "As much as that feedback stung, I knew immediately that it was true. This wasn't an anomaly; it was the way I had often acted under duress. Feeling a sense of control helped me work through stressful situations. I didn't trust my teammates, and I didn't understand, or even ask for, anyone else's point of view." Katie had heard some of this feedback before but had not previously taken it to heart: "Receiving this feedback in a classroom setting allowed me to reflect on it differently, and it changed me. The strength of my own beliefs, and the way they drove me to behave even in such a low-stakes situation, became profoundly apparent. Once my beliefs about my own sense of control, and mistrust in others changed, then my behaviors changed. It really changed the way I approached work, and my newer behaviors have been much more successful in working with others."

Christopher Held, a former MYLO student and a Fortune 500 senior executive, told me that "I took a new job after several years at a major strategy-consulting firm. I felt like I knew what I was doing." But there was someone on Chris's team who would question his opinions, assessments, and decisions. "I used to classify people as those I thought were friendly, and supportive of my work, and those that were combative, those that didn't seem very supportive. So I classified this guy as combative and was combative right back."

Later, Chris was going through a difficult situation at work, one in which his own boss was unhelpful and had intimated that Chris's job could be at risk because of it. Plus, he had a new baby on the way. The man whom Chris had earlier classified as a combatant turned out to be one of the most helpful people during that time. According to Chris, "One day he stopped by my office and said, 'Come on, we're going to go watch some football.' And that's what we did. He had me over to his house to watch football and help me get my mind off all the things that were stressing me out. During the discussion, I mentioned that I'd always thought he was 'against' me, so was surprised at how kind he was at this time." It turned out that Chris's colleague classified himself as strongheaded, telling Chris that if he disagreed with someone, he made it very clear and asked them to prove their point—he wouldn't agree with their assessment or decision just because they were smart, more senior, or a nice person. He wanted to be convinced.

"This was such an eye-opener for me," Chris said. "It made me realize that this person was actually helping me get better, helping me to sharpen my argument. It also made me realize that I'd been projecting myself as this big deal, and here he was being very human and very kind to me when it felt like my world was falling apart. It had been my own behaviors that made us butt heads. It took me a while to realize that I was projecting myself in the wrong way and that this way was going to make people respond negatively to what I'm doing and saying."

In addition to helping us understand how our behaviors affect others and the way they respond to us, self-reflection can have other significant benefits. For example, connecting with our values and better understanding who and whose thinking has shaped us, as well as our definition of success, can inform important career choices, as the next two stories demonstrate.

Beat Buhlmann is an interim CIO for a big international company in Switzerland: "I chose to go into interim management, including doing business turnarounds, because I like project-based work and in this type of work you come in, you analyze, you get it fixed, and you don't have to deal with a lot of political games. You're in and out in three to four months. It suits me well, and it allows me to have a lot more freedom. My son is eleven now. In a couple of years, he'll be an adult and go his own way. So I may not want to do this once he's an adult. I want to do all of this now because I can take a summer break and have six weeks of summer break with him. If I worked for most corporations, I couldn't do this."

Daniel Mouen Makoua, a London-based leader of a global environmental services company, told me about how many of his earliest influences have affected his career choices: "I was very influenced by my father, who asked me to look after the people in our village, which is near Douala in Cameroon.

From him, I learned about purpose, a sense of responsibility, and a duty of care, particularly looking after people that are less privileged. From my mother, who is French and came from a humble background of growing up during World War II, I learned determination, innovation, pragmatism, and resilience. And a close family friend, who grew up in the same village as my father, later became the minister of finance in Cameroon. From him, I learned to think at a strategic level and the role one should play in the management of a country. I also took from him that finance is where the power is, which influenced me in my career choice."

After a long career in finance, all these influences came together for Daniel: "I wanted to restore nature and started a company to do just that. This commitment to people, and by extension nature, is the guiding principle of our company. We apply it diligently whether with rural communities in Scotland, Native American nations in Virginia or Minnesota, or across Africa. This brings together all of my early influences—the sense of purpose, the duty of care, the pragmatism, the determination and innovation, and even the finance—aimed at improving the world. It's all come full circle."

Not Everyone Benefits from the Questions

I've shared the Six Questions for Self-Understanding with countless people from a variety of backgrounds and industries, and I have found an obvious pattern. Those who spend more time on the questions get more out of them. And those who rush through the questions or who refuse to engage with the questions do not benefit from the insights they may have gained.

Christine, an entrepreneur, came to the MYLO program in search of some answers about how to get people on board with her vision so that she could take her business to the next level. Before the start of the session, she approached to tell me about her business and how she'd bootstrapped it and opened a new outlet in an iconic New York location. She then went on to tell me how hard it was to keep employees, how no one seemed to "get it," and that she wanted to learn some tricks and techniques to better manage her team. When we got to the Six Questions for Self-Understanding, Christine balked. She spent a few moments writing, then picked up her phone to check her messages. I walked over and gently encouraged her to spend more time delving into the questions, writing whatever came to her without editing, and to try to pay attention to the feedback she'd received over the years because there might be some good insights there. She gave me an annoyed look, sighed, and then picked up her pen again to begin writing. When I looked up a few minutes later, Christine was back on her phone, so I tried once more to encourage her to delve more deeply into the questions. She replied curtly that she had, then got up and left the room, phone in hand.

Throughout the rest of the program, Christine participated in discussions, often complaining about her many problem employees and asking for specific advice on how to convince others to adopt her way of doing things. Whatever the problem she was facing, it seemed that it was always someone else's fault. During the breakout activities, she dominated discussions, argued with others about why her way was the right way, had an opinion on everyone else's ideas, and rarely listened to or really heard what others had to say. By the end of the program, it was clear why Christine had so many problems on her team. She not only didn't understand herself well, or how she came across to others, but was also unwilling to do the hard work of looking for insight into her situation and how her own behaviors might have been contributing to her unhappy situation.

Although Christine got very little from the program, her behaviors helped others by showing them how someone with a lack of self-understanding and self-management came across to others. As one participant told me later, "It was a master class in how I don't want to behave."

Leadership Takes Courage, and Courage Comes from Clarity

Your differences are what allow you to lead differently than others. The best way for each of us to lead is from our clarity about who we are and what we want to do with our time on Earth. As Coco Chanel once said, "To be irreplaceable, you must be different." You are different from others, and that is a good thing. Understanding that we are different from others helps us make decisions that are right for us, as opposed to those that sound right from society's perspective or anyone else's. It helps us choose our behaviors and actions more carefully on our way to becoming the leader we want to be. It's from understanding ourselves that we gain clarity about who we are and who we want to become. From this clarity we gain the courage to become the person we want to be, the leader *only* we can be. You are unique, and that is a good thing.

4

Managing Yourself

IMANI ENTERED THE ROOM ON the second day of our executive program and walked toward me with her phone in hand and a "wait till you see this" look on her face. As she got closer, she extended her arm and showed me what was on the screen. An email. She then handed me the phone and asked me to read the email.

It was addressed to about ten people, including Imani, and it had a two-word subject line: Bad Mood. This was followed, in the body of the email, by "Team, I'm not in a good mood today, so please excuse me if I dispense with the pleasantries" and then signed by someone named Beth.

"That's my boss," said Imani with her eyebrows raised, "and that's an email we get several times a year, and when we do, we all brace for a day that's probably going to put us all in a bad mood too. When Beth sends an email like this, she's not only going to dispense with the pleasantries; she's going to bark at people in meetings, vent her frustration about everything that bothers her, and be short-tempered when we can't immediately intuit what she wants. On most days when she sends an email like this, she's downright mean and nasty, and we all try to avoid her because when you do have to interact with her, you walk away feeling as if you've been rubbed by sandpaper." Imani rolled her eyes and shook her head.

Bad Mood Beth is a classic example of someone who has enough self-understanding to know they're in a bad mood but who lacks the skills to manage themselves through the bad mood, leaving others to suffer the consequences. Understanding ourselves is the foundation of effective leadership, but it's only the starting point—we also need to envision the leader we want to become and then manage ourselves toward that future state.

In this chapter we'll discuss the leader you want to become, the New You, and the hard work of replacing a habitual way of reacting with a new behavior that gets you closer to your goal. You decide the leader you want to become, and the impact you want to have, and then make it so. This is easier said than done, of course, and in this chapter we'll delve into the "how to" of self-management, the obstacles that can get in the way, and how to address these obstacles. This chapter should come with two warnings: (1) "Hard work ahead" and (2) "This is where many people stop because of the hard work of self-management." I'm guessing that you are not afraid of the hard work.

From Self-Understanding to Self-Management

Leadership emerges from your life story and is honed through intention. Now that you understand yourself at a deeper level, the metamorphosis of intentionally evolving toward the leader you desire to become can truly begin. When you know where you want to go, how you define success, and what you are willing to do to achieve that success, you enter the realm of self-determination. While answering the Six Questions for Self-Understanding in Chapter 3, you gained insight into your values and aspirations, as well as who and what have influenced you over the years, events that helped shape you, and how your actions and behaviors affect others. And in Chapter 1 you began thinking about the leader you are now, the leader you'd like to become, and what skills and behaviors you may need to master to become that leader. Self-understanding gives us insight, but self-management helps us get there. Altering the way we behave changes the way people perceive and respond to us, and can change the way we think and feel about ourselves. With time and practice, the new behavior becomes a more natural component of our leadership style and way of being. This, in turn, has a transformative effect on our own leadership abilities as well as the product of the work we do with and through others.

We can choose whether we want to react to what is in front of us, as we have done in the past, or whether we'd like to have a more conscious, deliberate, helpful response: "Between stimulus and response there is a space. In that space is our power to choose our response. In our response lies our growth and our freedom." Often attributed to Viktor Frankl, Austrian psychiatrist and psychotherapist, Holocaust survivor, and author of *Man's Search for Meaning*, this idea gets at how we begin to change our behavior toward one that better suits our new identity and our new way of being.

To have the desired impact, our behaviors must align with our intentions. For example, if we want to increase innovation and creative ideas in our team, we may choose to solicit others' ideas for how to solve a problem or point out the positives in ideas they offer, rather than offering our ideas first or being quick to point out the flaws in others' ideas. Or if we want to become a better listener, we may allow people to finish their thoughts before responding, or ask more questions to make sure we understand their perspective, rather than interrupting them or assuming we understand the situation well enough to offer advice. Self-management is hard work that may involve many mistakes as we learn a new behavior or skill, yet it leads to much better results. Just as I went through in learning to speak up in meetings. Or as Phil did in realizing he had become a leader even he didn't like, refining what being a leader meant to him, and then rerouting his behaviors in that direction.

With self-management, you are not trying to change your *personality*. You are trying to change your *behavior*. Executive coach Jennifer Porter describes self-management as "a conscious choice to resist a preference or habit, and instead demonstrate a more productive behavior."[1] Our behaviors are a choice, a deliberate choice. And with all choices come consequences.

Self-management is about making intentional choices about the actions and behaviors that will move us closer to our goals. The Managing Yourself Model (Figure 4.1) depicts this. First, we do the work of self-understanding, going back into our past experiences and influences, looking internally for how they shaped us, and better understanding our values, emotional awareness, and definition of success. This gives us insight about ourselves and what matters to us. At this point, we move into the realm of self-management.

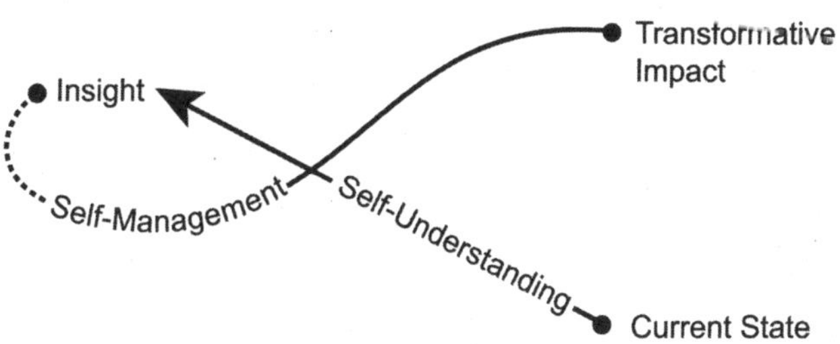

Figure 4.1. The Managing Yourself Model

Self-management begins with intention, when we decide what type of leader we want to become. Next, we determine what it will take to become this leader, in particular the behaviors and skills that will get us closer to our desired way of being. Last, we work on these new behaviors until we become more proficient at them and they become a natural part of our leadership style. As with the S curve, when developing a new skill or behavior, we get better slowly, then quickly, and this leads to transformative results.

This can be a messy process, and there will be times when we revert to old behaviors or don't do well, as Shaun Carver, executive director of International House at the University of California, Berkeley, found: "It's so easy to backslide. For most of my life I've been impatient with situations, with other people, and with myself, and I've worked hard to change this." When I asked him how he's approached this change, he told me three things:

> The first adjustment I made was to change my expectations about time. In one place I used to work, it was completely manic and everyone had too much going on, so everyone was impatient about everything. There were a lot of crises, which led to a lot of burnout. Then I went to work for another organization that was on the other end of the spectrum—it felt like everything happened in slow motion and nothing was urgent. So now, I'm setting my expectations at a happy medium for myself, and my staff has really helped with this—we want to make change, and we want to see progress, but not everything is an emergency. Second, I've thought a lot about what type of organization I want to create. I don't want it to be a ready-shoot-aim and burnout culture like the first organization, nor do I want it to be a ready-ready-ready and countdown to retirement like the other organization. I'm looking for that measured approach

> and moving at the appropriate pace. And lastly, I'm learning to be kind to myself, which helps me be more patient, and more present, with others. I've learned over the years to be more like this, but sometimes I backslide and don't do it as well as I'd like.

It takes intention, time, and effort to develop new skills and behaviors, including sticking with the process and continuing to come back to our intention and practice of the new behavior.

We are always in the process of becoming, and long-term success comes through a series of these intentional skill- and behavior-development efforts. Once we've mastered a new behavior, we have a higher level of impact. We ourselves have evolved by learning this new skill or behavior, and this allows us to have better results. We are getting closer to the leader we want to become. At this point, it's time to launch a new round of self-reflection, insight, and targeted improvement. Upleveling our skills and behaviors is an ongoing process: Each new level of leadership requires a new level of us. In many respects, we transform ourselves at each new level of leadership, and this growth puts us on track to uplevel our skills and behaviors again and again (and again). This is how we continue to evolve as a leader: through an ongoing, deliberate series of choices about who we are and want to become (see Figure 4.2).

There are a variety of skills and behaviors that make us effective leaders. And although understanding strategy and

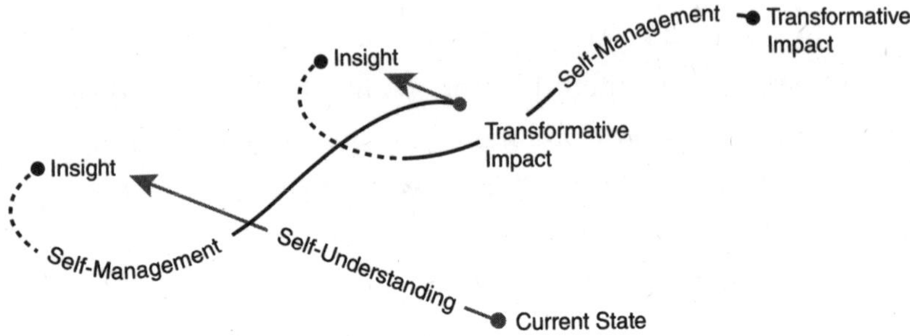

Figure 4.2. The Ongoing Cycle of Transformative Impact

finance may help us throughout our career, most of the skills and behaviors that come up in the MYLO program have to do with interpersonal skills and, more specifically, with understanding and managing the emotions that drive our behavior.

The Role of Emotions in Self-Management

Often, our development as a leader depends on more effective emotional regulation. And just as we need to understand ourselves in order to manage ourselves, we need to understand our own emotions in order to manage them. Once again, we can't manage something we aren't aware of or don't understand.

You may consider yourself a highly emotional person or someone who's not emotional at all, but the fact is that we are all having emotions all the time. It's part of what makes us human. The question is whether you're managing your emotions or whether your emotions are managing you. We're often told in the workplace, and even in families, that emotions are best left out of the discussion or decision. However, as humans, this isn't possible because each of us comes fully equipped with a range of emotions that are with us all the time. All. The. Time. For example, you may feel anxious that becoming a more effective leader may involve getting more comfortable with your emotions, or feel angry that we're even talking about emotions within this book, or feel bored because you know all of this already.

What are emotions? According to psychologist Paul Ekman, "Emotions are a process, a particular kind of automatic appraisal influenced by our evolutionary and personal past, in which we sense that something important to our welfare is occurring, and a set of psychological changes and emotional behaviors begins to deal with the situation." In other words, emotions are natural, involuntary responses to a stimulus. We have a subjective experience, then a physiological response, then a behavioral response.[2]

To get a sense of this, let's do a quick exercise. Look toward the door in whatever room you're in. Now imagine that the door is closed, and it begins to open very slowly. As the door continues to open, after a few seconds of anticipation, you see that what is behind the door and is about to enter the room is a bear. Not the cute character Winnie the Pooh or a teddy bear, but a big grizzly bear, an *Ursus arctos horribilis*, one that stands more than six feet tall and might weigh up to eight hundred pounds. Imagine this grizzly walking into the room where you are right now. What emotion might you have? Close your eyes, imagine this scenario, and see what emotion comes up for you. Do you feel anything in your body? If so, take note of it and feel that feeling.

Typical responses to this question include "terror," "fear," "surprise," and "panic." And these would be apt words because a bear is big, has long claws and powerful jaws, and could hurt you. These emotions are alerting you to a potential danger, a threat in your environment.

Now look back at the door in the room you're in and imagine the closed door slowly opening again. After a few seconds of anticipation, as the door continues to open, you see that it's the person you love most in this world about to enter the room. What emotions might you have seeing this? Typical responses here include "joy," "happiness," "relief," and "serenity." Do you feel anything in your body this time? If so, take note of it and feel *this* feeling.

Whether it's the grizzly bear or the person you most love who enters the room, you had an emotional response to a stimulus. Two different situations, seeing either a bear or the person you love most in this world, evoke very different emotions. And you don't need to actually see a bear or the person you love to feel these emotions—in this situation you only *imagined* that you saw them.

Often, people tell me that their chest got tight or their heart beat faster when they were thinking about the bear and that their shoulders relaxed and they began to smile when thinking about the person they loved coming through the door. These different emotions become feelings when we feel them in our body. In fact, emotions and feelings are tightly linked—the emotion is an unconscious, unbidden reaction to a stimulus. And when we feel it in our body, we call it a feeling—because we *feel* the emotion.

We have emotions because of some stimulus, and the stimulus doesn't have to be something physical that happens or even something that happens in the moment. Emotions can also arise from thinking about the past (e.g., remembering a wonderful vacation or an ugly argument) or the future (e.g., anticipation or dread about an upcoming event). For example, think of the emotion you might have if your boss came by and said, "Please come see me in my office." You might feel happy anticipation if she was smiling and looked happy, or you might feel a sense of dread if she looked concerned or angry.

Although psychologists disagree on the exact number of basic emotions, there are some that appear in most lists of emotions, including anger, disgust, fear, happiness, sadness, and surprise. Some of these emotions may be more pleasant for you than others, but all of them serve a purpose:

- **Anger** motivates us to take action when we believe our path to a goal has been blocked, a boundary has been violated, or we (or others) have been wronged.
- **Disgust** alerts us to what may be unhealthy or harmful to us so that we can avoid it.

- **Fear** helps us stay safe by alerting us to potential danger so that we can take action to avoid that danger.
- **Happiness** helps us notice and move toward who and what provide us pleasure and give us a sense of well-being.
- **Sadness** focuses us on what matters and helps us slow down to feel our losses, connect with others, and show others we need support.
- **Surprise** directs our attention to something unexpected to determine what is going on and whether it is dangerous.[3]

Emotions are data alerting us to something in our internal or external environment, and to what we may need in that moment. However, as Susan David, the author of *Emotional Agility*, likes to remind us, "Emotions are data, not directives."[4] If we recognize the emotion we're having, we don't need to follow what it seems to be urging us to do. For example, if someone says something in a meeting that makes you feel angry, you may want to yell at that person. However, this behavior may be inappropriate in that meeting, and it may be more productive for you to calm yourself in the moment and address the person who made the comment sometime after the meeting. We may not control the stimulus or the physiological response, but we have more control over our behavioral response.

The Bridge Between Self-Understanding and Self-Management

But how can we manage our emotional responses? By paying attention. Mindfulness, the practice of paying attention without judgment to what is happening in the present moment, is the bridge between understanding ourselves and managing ourselves. It's the bridge between our intentions and our behaviors. This means both understanding what our intentions are and being aware of those intentions in various situations, in those moments when our choice of behavior really matters (see Figure 4.3).

Mindfulness Is the Bridge Between Self-Understanding and Self-Management

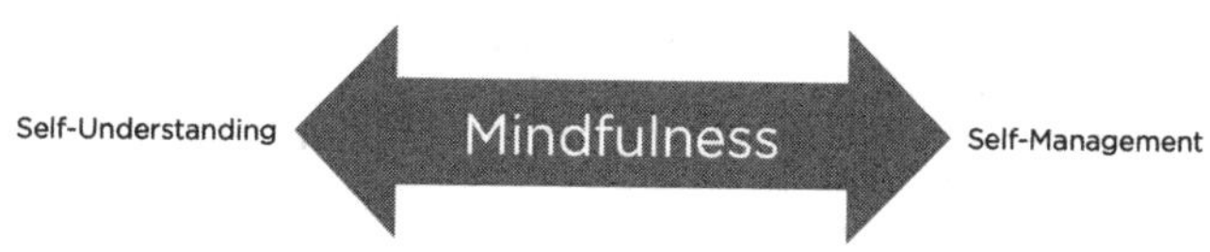

Figure 4.3. The Bridge Between Self-Understanding and Self-Management

When we're mindful, we're paying attention to what is going on in the present moment rather than thinking about what we should have said, what's on our phones, or what we'll say or do next. In one of my executive programs, someone told the story about how when his kids tell his wife that Dad had agreed to what they asked for, his wife asks the kids, "Was your father on his phone when he said that?" She knows that sometimes he's so absorbed in his phone, so distracted by it, that he says yes without really processing the question and what would be an appropriate response. It's an automated, unthinking reaction—the opposite of responding mindfully.

Being mindful involves noticing what is in front of you, what is around you, or the emotions inside you in the moment, without judgment. It sounds so simple, yet it is not. This might mean noticing the look on a person's face or their body language while you are talking to them. Or it might involve noticing that you are feeling angry because your boss just told you there is a problem in some part of the supply chain, and you'll need to work over the weekend to fix the problem. It takes practice to become more mindful.

You can start by choosing an activity you do every day, such as making coffee, brushing your teeth in the morning, or getting dressed. Pay attention to what you're doing and what you observe. For example, rather than thinking about your day ahead as you make coffee, hear the sound of opening the coffee container; smell the coffee beans; feel the texture of the bean grinder; hear the sound of the beans hitting the inside of the bean grinder; notice the sound of the grinder and how the sound changes as the beans are ground more finely; hear the muffled sound of the coffee hitting the filter; notice the sound of the water being poured into the coffee machine; notice the sounds, smells, and sights as the coffee goes through the machine; feel the weight and coolness of the coffee mug; hear the sound of the coffee being poured into your coffee mug; notice how the mug gets hot as you pour the coffee into it; feel the coffee in your mouth and taste the bitterness (or sweetness or smoothness) of the coffee. Use all your senses. Pay attention to what you're doing, hearing, seeing, smelling, touching/feeling, and tasting, and if your mind wanders (which it will), bring yourself back to the activity you're performing. It takes some practice to do this, and you'll find that, as with any new skill, you'll get better at it slowly, then quickly.

Emotional Regulation

Our behaviors very often relate to not being aware of the emotions we're having, and if we're not aware of whatever emotion we're having, we can't manage it. If your answer to Question 5 in Chapter 3, about the extent to which you are aware of—and allow yourself to feel—your emotions, was "not much" or "I don't know," or whether you can point to some unexpected feedback, particularly feedback you disagreed with, in Question 6, please pay close attention to this section. These answers indicate that you may not be aware of your emotions and how they affect others. And even if you answered the above questions differently, consider the possibility that you may not be as emotionally self-aware as you think. In fact, most of us are not self-aware. According to researcher Tasha Eurich, "Although 95 percent of people think they're self-aware, only 10 to 15 percent actually are."[5] This means that most of us are not only unaware of our own emotions, but we also don't understand how our emotions affect others and therefore shape others' perceptions about us.

Sometimes our behaviors relate to being aware of our emotions but not being able to manage that emotion. Like Bad Mood Beth. When we have an emotion, particularly one of the more challenging emotions like anger, sadness, or jealousy, we may need to take care about where, when, and how we express that emotion. This calls for emotional regulation, also known as emotional management or emotional agility. According to psychologist Steven Stosny, behavioral self-regulation is "the ability to act in your long-term best interest, consistent with your deepest values."[6]

To become more adept at emotional regulation, begin by becoming more mindful of your emotions. One simple practice is to set a timer for multiple times each day to ask yourself what you're feeling in each of these moments and then closing your eyes briefly to feel the emotion, perhaps pinpointing where you feel it in your body. This can be difficult at first, for most of us are not used to paying attention to our emotions. However, after doing this for several days, it becomes easier and more natural, and you may find yourself becoming more aware of the emotions you are experiencing even when you don't consciously stop to feel them. You can also put a sticky note on your computer with the word "Emotion?" on it to remind yourself to check in with the emotion you're feeling in that moment. Do this multiple times each day, and it will become easier over time and, more importantly, will make it more likely that you'll be able to understand and manage a challenging emotion when it comes up.

As you become aware of your emotions, do as UCLA professor of psychiatry Dan Siegel has said: "Name it to tame it." Just naming the emotion we're having helps us not only understand the emotion but also begin to take the power away from some of the more challenging emotions like disappointment, fear, and regret. When you start naming your emotions, try to pinpoint not just the emotion but also the intensity of the emotion. For example, when we feel anger, we might feel irritated or we might feel infuriated—both these emotions are in the anger "family," but they feel different to the person experiencing that emotion. Table 4.1 displays three common emotions—anger, fear, and happiness—and five words describing each of these emotions, listed from lower to higher intensity. To expand your understanding of emotions, you can create your own list of emotions or download a longer list of emotions and various words to describe them from my website (www.margaretandrews.com/mylobookresources). You may have a different ordering, from less intense to more intense, and that's fine. The important thing is that you can identify and understand the emotion you're having.

The next step in emotional regulation is to begin accepting your emotions. We may not *enjoy* feeling certain emotions, such as anxiety, envy, or sadness, but the truth is that sometimes we do feel these emotions. Someone once mentioned

Anger	Fear	Happiness
Displeased	Uneasy	Content
Annoyed	Apprehensive	Lighthearted
Angry	Fearful	Happy
Exasperated	Panicked	Joyful
Enraged	Petrified	Euphoric

Table 4.1. The Different Words Used to Describe Various Emotions

to me that the word *emotion* has the word *motion* contained within it, which is a good reminder that emotions are meant to move through us. Rather than trying to ignore or suppress difficult emotions, which only keeps them present and active within us, accept an emotion for what it is, the emotion you're having in that moment, to loosen its grip on you and allow it to move through you.

Next, after becoming more aware and accepting of your emotions, you can begin to set your intentions for your behaviors in general and in any given situation. For example, you may have a difficult employee and find yourself frustrated and angry when they repeatedly make the same mistake, are late to the meeting *again*, or don't deliver on their promises. If you would like to be more measured in your response in these situations, you can set that as your intention. Then you can envision a difficult encounter with that employee and how you would like to respond in that encounter rather than reacting the way you have in the past. You can also think of multiple ways of responding to their behavior (e.g., yelling at them, rolling your eyes, trying to understand their perspective, stopping to ask them how they're doing, showing them support rather than frustration, or any other way you might respond to this situation). Envision each of these scenarios and choose responses that may work well during the actual encounter, a response that fits your intention and gets you closer to your long-term goal. If possible, practice this response out loud or, even better, by role-playing the scenario with a trusted colleague or friend. Thinking ahead about this and practicing your response can help you choose a more productive behavior when you are in the moment because you've already thought about it.

When in a situation where you want to regulate your emotions and choose a more helpful behavior, pay attention to the emotions you're having in the moment, and be mindful of your intentions. From the earlier steps on becoming more familiar with your emotions, being able to name them, and accepting them, you'll now be in a better position to be aware of your emotions in all kinds of situations, including very intense, challenging situations such as a difficult negotiation, having to give a negative performance review, being on the receiving end of bad news, or a variety of other difficult scenarios. Although this can take some time to get better at and we are all prone to occasional backsliding, understanding the emotions you're feeling in the moment and understanding your intentions for how you behave during the encounter will help you respond with a more helpful behavior rather than reacting with an unhelpful behavior.

When you find yourself in a difficult situation or experiencing a strong, challenging emotion, you can take a moment to collect yourself. This may come in the form of taking a drink from your water bottle, taking a deep breath, or verbalizing a reaction you're having, such as saying, "Wow!" or "I wonder why you would say that?" and then being quiet to listen to the response. Or you might say, "I need a moment to process that," and then take that moment. This can slow down the situation and give you, as well as other people, the space to choose a response more carefully rather than simply reacting.

To better understand and manage your emotions, take time to reflect on how you have presented as a leader in various situations. For example, on a daily basis you might reflect on how the day went and what went well and what you might want to do differently the next day. Or, after a difficult conversation, reflect on the emotions you were feeling, the behaviors you exhibited, how you think others in the conversation were feeling, how you think the encounter went, and what you want to keep in mind for future encounters like this. Reflection helps you internalize the lesson and apply it going forward.

Emotional regulation is hard. And it becomes more difficult when some of our basic needs for sleep, nutritious food, and exercise aren't being met. Most of us are not at our best when we are tired or hungry, and we are therefore more likely to react (often poorly) to whatever situation we are in rather than responding deliberately with behaviors that are aligned with our goals. And exercise helps us self-manage because it alleviates stress and increases positive emotions.

According to philosopher, psychologist, and physician William James, "Action seems to follow feeling, but really action and feeling go together; and by regulating the action, which is under the more direct control of the will, we can indirectly regulate the feeling, which is not."[7] Self-regulation allows us to feel one way and behave another way by being aware of our longer-term goal and molding our behavior toward that goal.

The Challenges in Managing Ourselves—What Gets in the Way

There are two important challenges in self-management that can make it difficult for us to evolve toward the transformational impact we seek. The first is our fear of vulnerability; the second is our understanding a concept and how to implement that concept but not actually following through on that implementation, also known as the knowing-doing gap.

Fear of Vulnerability

Working on new behaviors can be hard and make us feel vulnerable, a feeling that most of us do not enjoy. Our anxieties, fear of looking foolish, and fear of failure are often what hold us back from engaging with new behaviors. Change, including learning a new behavior, is hard for most people because it pushes us out of our comfort zone. However, our growth begins only once we step outside our comfort zone. And as we discussed in Chapter 2 with S curves, many people abandon learning a new behavior because of feeling vulnerable when they make mistakes and instead double down on what made them successful (e.g., intelligence, hard skills, hard work), but this doesn't bring them to the next level.

When learning new skills, we will often be outside our comfort zone, and it's in this zone of discomfort where our growth happens. Marian Poirier, a senior executive for a global financial services firm in Australia, has, as she told me, "become addicted to being uncomfortable." She wasn't always this way, though:

> I'm someone that enjoys one-on-one interactions and used to really dislike giving speeches. But several years ago I joined a local board for people working in financial services, and part of my role was doing presentations and emceeing events. In the beginning it was nerve-racking to put myself out there, but over time I not only got used to doing these things—I actually got to be good at them, and the more I did these things, the more confident I became. And after a few years of this, it was time to take on a new challenge, so I decided to move out of my comfort zone yet again by

joining the board of the CFA Society of New South Wales, which was mostly made up of C-suite executives. I was often uncomfortable as I found my point of view frequently differed and, once I accepted this as a good thing, I embraced it and was, I believe, appreciated more because of it. It was from these experiences, really pushing myself to do things that were outside my comfort zone, that I learned I actually enjoy getting uncomfortable. It means I'm learning something new, and it's quite exciting. If I'm not uncomfortable, it means I'm not pushing myself, not learning, not growing. And since I like to learn and continue to grow, I've learned to embrace that discomfort.

Knowing-Doing Gap

The hard part isn't knowing what to do; it's doing it. Although Bad Mood Beth likely knows she shouldn't treat people the way she does on those bad-mood days, she can't manage herself well enough to enact what she knows, which is a great example of the knowing-doing gap, when we know something yet don't do it. We don't get credit for knowing we should think before we speak; we get credit for thinking before we speak. We don't get credit for knowing we should take care of ourselves, including eating well, sleeping well, and moving more, to show up as the leader we want to be; we get credit for doing these things and showing up as that leader. Knowing what to do is easy; doing it is hard. Managing ourselves goes beyond knowing what we should do to actually applying what we know.

Researchers have found that working to bridge the gap between what we know about leadership and how we behave leads to more positive emotions such as relief, satisfaction, happiness, and pride.[8] Learning new behaviors and skills also increases our self-efficacy, our belief that we have the capacity to solve difficult problems. Solving one problem or mastering a new skill or behavior gives us confidence that we can solve other problems or master other new skills and behaviors.

Designing—and Becoming—the New You

Designing the New You is an act of imagination. What type of leader do you want to become? For this exercise, which should take between ten and twenty minutes, please go back to your answers to the questions in Chapter 1—in particular, your answers to the second question (What type of leader would you like to become?) and the third question (What is the difference between the leader you want to be and the leader you are now?).

Now, more fully envision the leader you want to become. Get a deep, clear picture in your mind of you as that leader. You may want to use phrasing such as "I am someone who . . . ," "I am the type of person who . . . ," "I am a leader who . . . ," or "As a leader, I . . ." to help you in this exercise. This is the person you are deciding to become. What do you look like? How is your body language? What does your voice, or tone of voice, sound like? How do you interact with others? How do they respond to you? How do you feel as this leader? How do you make others feel? What is it that you're doing that makes them feel this way? Write down your answers to these questions. Notice what it would feel like to become this person.

Next, think of a challenging situation or person you are currently facing. It might be a difficult and demanding boss, an employee who may need to be removed from the team, a client that is making unreasonable demands, or something else entirely. Choose a difficult scenario or interaction that is important to you, and imagine how the New You might approach the situation, what intent the New You might have for the interaction, and how the New You might behave during the encounter. Let your vision of the New You, how you want to be, guide your actions and behaviors. How would this person behave in this situation? Now behave that way in your mind. Envision it. Feel it.

It may be helpful to remember that you do not need to be confined by your past or present circumstances or behaviors. You are designing your future, and although it will be built upon everything in your life to date, it is a *deliberate choice* for how you want to be in the future. To get different results, we need different approaches and behaviors. As Leonard Cohen once said, "Act the way you want to be and soon you will be the way you act." We feel differently when we behave in new ways and see people respond to our new behaviors differently than the way they responded to our previous behaviors.

Becoming the New You is an act of intention, and this is where self-management comes in. We don't magically become better at listening, delegating, perspective taking, managing difficult conversations, or building relationships—we have to manage our behaviors toward these goals. Let the New You guide your development. Keep in mind that discomfort from behaving in new ways is a sign of growth. When you stumble, and you will if you are embarking on an ambitious goal, take the lesson and get back up and try again.

Tips for Self-Management

There are several mindsets and practices that can help you become more effective at self-management, including these:

- **Set yourself up for success** by getting enough sleep, eating nutritious food, getting some exercise each day, and refraining from multitasking, which exhausts your brain.
- **Recognize that what got you to this level of success won't get you to your next level of success and that to continue to improve, you will need to learn new skills and behaviors.** Different levels of leadership require enhanced versions of ourselves. It's not that we are defective; it's that we all have areas where we can improve.
- **Tell other people what new behaviors you're working on.** Not only will they be able to give you

feedback on what's working, but you will also be modeling improvement for them.

- **Search for role models.** Who do you know who does this well? Observe what they do and how they behave, and try out those actions and behaviors yourself. If you know the person, you might talk to them and ask for insights and advice on developing those behaviors.
- **Consider using an alter ego, or persona.** Many artists and athletes use alter egos to help them channel their behaviors a certain way, including Beyoncé (Sasha Fierce), the late Kobe Bryant (Black Mamba), and Eminem (Slim Shady). Todd Herman, author of *The Alter Ego Effect,* writes that "the idea of using Alter Egos to create some distance between how you currently see yourself and how you'd like to perform" allows you to bridge the gap between the Current You and the New You.[9] For example, you might think about how Superman would approach a situation, or Wonder Woman, Babe Ruth, Charles Darwin, Julius Caesar, James Bond, or Eleanor Roosevelt, or a cat. Using an alter ego allows you to step into, or become, that person or idea as you are learning a new way of behaving.
- **Reflect.** Spending time reflecting on our actions and behaviors can help us become more self-aware about how our actions and behaviors affect others, as well as when we are experiencing a knowing-doing gap

and not enacting a behavior we know would be more helpful.

- **Celebrate progress.** We can expect to feel vulnerable as we learn new skills and make mistakes in front of others and encounter hiccups and setbacks as we progress. Don't wait for perfection—celebrate the progress.

The New You Is a Work in Progress

We are all a work in progress. We are always in the process of becoming. Remember that you are learning and that there will be shortfalls and downfalls along the way. This is to be expected. Keep your eyes on the prize, ask for advice, ask for feedback (and listen to it), and keep at it: Keep practicing your new behaviors, your new ways of behaving and being. You are in the process of becoming the leader you want to become, and it is well within your ability to change. It's a process. And it takes time.

PART TWO

Leading Others

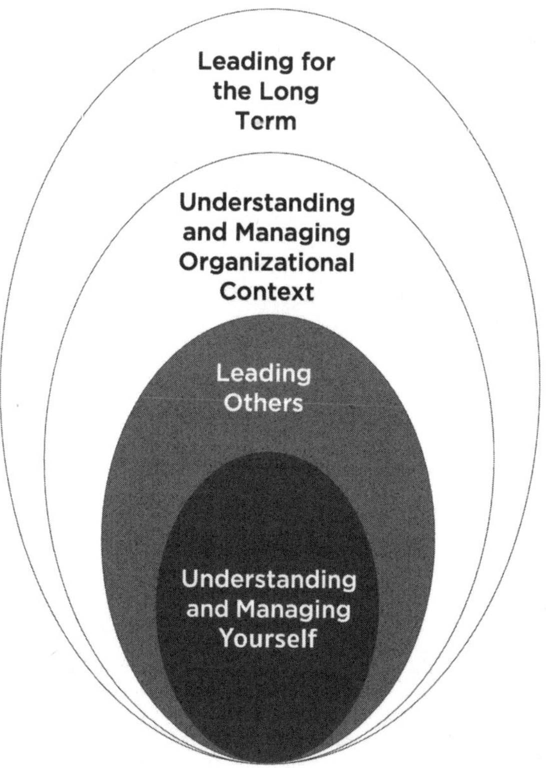

5

Leading Others

"I WORK IN A COMPANY with an open-office plan, where no one has a designated office and we all sit in a large room with rows of long tables," Sharon, a senior manager in a consumer-goods company, said in one of my executive programs, "and my right-hand person, Tara, sits at the table right behind me, so we are literally working back-to-back." When Sharon had a new idea, she would turn around, tap Tara on the shoulder, mention what she was thinking about, and ask Tara what she thought. They would discuss the idea for a minute or two, and then, later that day, Tara would come back with further thoughts and insights on what they'd discussed earlier.

"After this happened for a while, I realized that Tara and I had very different styles. I'm extraverted and like to talk through problems and solutions, and Tara is more introverted and likes to think through a problem before talking about it," Sharon said. Realizing this, she tried a different approach: "When I had something I wanted to discuss with Tara, rather than turning around to discuss it in the moment, I'd send her a message, telling her what I was thinking and asking if we could talk about it later that day. The results of doing it this way are significant—Tara comes to that discussion with more developed thoughts and ideas, we have a more robust discussion, and then I can take it from there. It turned out to be a much more effective approach."

At that point another program participant asked Sharon why she changed her approach since Tara worked for Sharon and should learn to adapt to Sharon's style, rather than the other way around. Sharon's answer was one of the best examples of understanding what is at the heart of effective leadership that I've heard: "It was a small change for me to make, and it really improved our results—so it was a great trade-off. My job as her manager isn't to get her to do things my way. It's to get the very best out of her."

Well said.

Leadership is, in many ways, a creative act. It involves working with people in all their individuality and complexity, and understanding how to get the best out of each person, as well as the collective team and larger organization. If you think back to your Best Boss, it's likely that the person you chose as your Best Boss showed genuine interest in you, which allowed them to connect with you and develop you to be a more effective version of yourself. Now it's our turn to do this for other people.

A Reason to Follow

Whether we're leading individuals, teams, the lab, a unit, a division, or a company, leadership begins with giving people a reason to follow us, which includes (a) a clear, compelling vision that is worthy of their talent and effort, and (b) a reason to work with us in achieving this vision.

A worthy goal, a strong sense of possibility, and a convincing plan for how to reach that goal are fundamental building blocks of leadership, as is helping people see their place in that vision. It gives people in the organization a shared sense of purpose, direction, and camaraderie in working to achieve that future. These are a few factors to consider in crafting and communicating a compelling vision:

- *Goal*: What are we trying to accomplish? What is our problem to solve?
- *Future state*: How will we know when we have succeeded? What will be different? Why is it worthy of the time and effort it will entail?
- *Effort*: What work needs to be done to achieve our goal? What changes will be necessary? Who will need to be involved in making this vision a reality? Who or what might impede our progress in achieving the goal?

In addition to communicating a vision or goal worthy of attention and commitment, people need a reason to trust *us* to lead them toward that vision. Part of their trust in us comes from our reputation as a leader, our track record of success, our credibility in tackling this specific issue, and how we present as a leader. If we have done the work in Chapters 3 and 4, we understand ourselves well, including who and what ideas and events have shaped us as an individual and how these influences show up in the way we lead, how we define success, how our behaviors have affected others, and our bedrock values. We also know the behaviors we are actively seeking to develop and are putting in the effort to become the leader we want to be. These new behaviors help us show up as predictable and reliable, so people we work with don't have to spend time, brainpower, or emotional energy trying to guess how we'll show up on any given day.

Understanding Others

Building a foundation of trust also entails letting others know that we want them to succeed and will do our best to help them succeed. And this begins by getting to know them.

Alex, who leads front- and back-office operations staff in a luxury hotel in New York City, one that has paparazzi waiting nearby to spot the celebrities, royalty, and business moguls who come and go from the hotel, told me about an early-career lesson he learned about leading others: "The man that hired me was a decent guy—smart, hardworking, and understood the business well, but he was very strict and not interested in getting to know the people who worked for him." This manager left for another job about six months after Alex arrived, and a new manager took over the unit. "This new manager was completely different from the first one—he got to know *everyone.* He not only knew their name, but he also knew where they were from, how many kids they had, the names of those kids, and even the dreams of those kids. He knew how long people had worked at the property, what they thought was going well and what could be improved. This manager took the time to make a personal connection with everyone on his team." According to Alex, the new manager's genuine interest in people made a big difference: "People had more pep in their step, and it felt more like a team. During peak periods, when we didn't have enough manpower to service the hotel and our guests, something that happens with some regularity in the hospitality industry, his style really showed its effectiveness. With the previous manager, no one would step up and volunteer to take on extra work, so the first boss had to assign that work, and people were rarely happy about it. With the second manager, people readily volunteered to work those extra shifts because they had more of a connection to him, to each other, and to the property. This was my first glimpse of what a really effective manager does, and the experience left a lasting impression on me." Alex incorporated this lesson into his own leadership style and credits his multiple promotions to the atmosphere he's created for his team and the success they've had because of it: "If people feel you understand and respect them, they will go the extra mile. In an industry like this, with a unionized workforce and a high degree of turnover, it makes all the difference." So simple, really.

Just as we are distinct individuals, so is each of the people who work with and for us. One of the best lessons I've learned about leadership came from having children. I have three of them, two boys and a girl, and prior to having my own, I'd spent very little time around kids, so I had no idea what I was doing when my first son was born. I had to learn everything about caring for an infant, including how to hold, feed, and clean him, but more importantly I had to learn about him as an individual. It was a steep learning curve for me, so when our second son arrived, I thought I had the parenting thing all figured out. But no. My second son was completely different from my first son. He had his own way of being, his own likes and dislikes, his own moods, and I had to learn to relate to him as a distinct individual, someone very different from his brother. Then my daughter came along, and I thought for sure, *now* I know something about raising kids! But no. Once again, this child was unlike the others, and I had to learn to relate to her as the unique individual she is. It shocked me how different each one of them is because they have the same parents and were raised in the same household. It was this experience that gave me real insight into the nature of leadership and changed the way I approached it: If my own children don't think and behave in the same way, why would I ever expect the random collection of diverse individuals at work to be similar in how they think and behave? Each person we work with is a unique individual, just like each one of our children or siblings, and just like us.

Ed Catmull, cofounder of Pixar and former president of Walt Disney Animation, expressed a similar thought in his bestselling book, *Creativity, Inc.* Catmull discusses leadership as a process that involves thinking creatively not only about business problems but also about the people solving those problems: "I can think of only one thing to compare it to: raising children. . . . To do either job well requires us to dig deeply within ourselves."[1] It also helps us to get to know each of our employees as the individual *they* are.

Just as understanding ourselves is the foundation of effective leadership, understanding the people we work with is the foundation of leading them. It's the basis for helping them to develop toward the leader only *they* can be. This benefits the individual, the team, and the organization in both the short term and the long term. It also benefits you and your reputation for developing others, which can also help your career. Adrienne, who was a senior vice president of marketing for a large mutual fund company, told me that "one of my favorite aspects of my work is helping my staff discover and develop their talents. And when I think they've grown as much as they can in my organization, I help them find a new challenge somewhere else at the firm." When I asked her if she was upset that people she had spent so much time and effort developing ended up moving on, she smiled and told me, "Not at all. It means that I have friends all over the organization. So when I need to get something done outside my group, I can often just pick up the phone and call one of my well-placed former team members to help me find the right person to talk to or to figure out how to remove an obstacle. I hadn't realized it at first, but investing in my people, which I did because I enjoyed it, actually had the secondary effect of paying career-long dividends for me."

Getting to know them as the individual they are helps you build a relationship. What is their background? What skills do they bring to the table? Which skills would they like to develop? What are their goals? Strengths? Areas for development? Interests? Motivators? How do they like to work?

Nadine Kawkabani, a strategy executive in a Boston-based financial services company, told me how and why she works to build a relationship with everyone on her staff: "I have a pretty diverse team, and when I bring someone onto the team, I go the extra mile to get to know them. I read books about their culture. I spend time with them. I invite them in. As their manager and colleague, I put the relationship first. I've always found that investing in people is the way to get the best out of them. Having a solid relationship means that we can have the conversations we need to have—sometimes some difficult conversations. They know that I care about them and have their back, so when I tell them they need to improve in certain areas, they know it comes from a good place."

Part of getting to know others is understanding what motivates them, and although we often default to thinking about money to motivate others, money is not always the prime motivator we think it is.[2] When I mentioned in a class several years ago that not everyone is motivated primarily by money, a hand shot up. When I called on Rodrigo, he said, "I don't believe it." He didn't believe that people were motivated at work by things beyond money. I then tried an experiment: I asked the class to raise their hand if they had ever turned down a job offer where they would have made more money or taken a new job where they made less money than the job they'd previously worked in. About one-third of the hands in the room went up, showing that many people in the room are motivated at work by things other than money. When I asked those people with their hands up what they cared about at work, other than money, they gave me a long list that included purpose, vision, reputation of the company, challenging work, community, autonomy in their work, collaboration, working with people they can learn from, a respectful environment, opportunity for creativity, a sense of belonging, and flexibility in how they do their work. I repeat this experiment several times each year, and the results are similar.

Many of these motivating factors are within our range of influence, and although it's not necessarily our job to motivate the people who work for us, it is our job to find out what motivates them and do our best to not *de*motivate them. Research also bears this out, finding that "employees who are intrinsically motivated are three times more engaged than employees who are extrinsically motivated (such as by money)" and that the people who focus on, and like, the work they do are more likely to enjoy their job.[3]

Part of understanding the people we work with is being aware of various aspects of their personality and how they like to work. I use a tool I like to share with my classes called a Zig-Zag chart (Figure 5.1), which helps us understand our style in approaching work and how this may be similar to or different from another person's style.

To use the tool, first go through and place an "X" in the circle along the continuum closest to where you are (e.g., are you more of an extravert or introvert, do you prefer to

The Zig-Zag Chart

Extraverted	○	○	○	○	○	○	○	○	○	○	Introverted
Analyze/Debate	○	○	○	○	○	○	○	○	○	○	Decide/Action
Big Picture	○	○	○	○	○	○	○	○	○	○	Details
Competitive	○	○	○	○	○	○	○	○	○	○	Collaborative
Critical of Others	○	○	○	○	○	○	○	○	○	○	Affirming of Others
Data-Driven	○	○	○	○	○	○	○	○	○	○	Intuition-Driven
Disciplined/Planful	○	○	○	○	○	○	○	○	○	○	Impulsive/Last-Minute
Task-Oriented	○	○	○	○	○	○	○	○	○	○	Relationship-Oriented
Encourage Conflict	○	○	○	○	○	○	○	○	○	○	Suppress Conflict
Even-Tempered	○	○	○	○	○	○	○	○	○	○	Moody
Goal-Oriented	○	○	○	○	○	○	○	○	○	○	Process-Oriented
Optimistic	○	○	○	○	○	○	○	○	○	○	Pessimistic
Organized	○	○	○	○	○	○	○	○	○	○	Disorganized
Pragmatic	○	○	○	○	○	○	○	○	○	○	Idealistic
Present-Focused	○	○	○	○	○	○	○	○	○	○	Future-Focused
Risk-Seeking	○	○	○	○	○	○	○	○	○	○	Risk-Avoiding

Figure 5.1. Work Style Differences: The Zig-Zag Chart

analyze and debate or decide and take action). Then draw your "zig-zag" by connecting your preferences. Then go back and put a different mark (e.g., a check ✓) for where you think the other person is along the continuum, and connect their zig-zag. What you can see now is in which areas you are close to them in style and where you are quite different. This helps you to better understand them and respond to them accordingly. As we learned from Sharon's story, sometimes getting to better outcomes involves bending our style to accommodate others. You can download a copy of the Zig-Zag chart at www.margaretandrews.com/mylobookresources or create one of your own.

In addition to getting to know people on your team, let them get to know you. Share what you're working on, why you're excited about the work you're doing, and what you do outside work (e.g., what books you read, a recent movie you enjoyed, a good restaurant you'd recommend, where you'd most like to travel). The goal is not to become their friend but rather to build a strong, trusting relationship. Having this relationship will help you to understand where they're coming from in discussions and why they may see things as they do, and it will also help them understand you and your perspective. Without a solid relationship, feedback and development conversations may feel (to them) like disapproval or an attack rather than the growth discussions you intend them to be. Let people know that you want them to be successful, and then help them do so.

Understanding Their Perspective

We all have our own perspective, our way of seeing the world. In Chapter 3 you had the opportunity to better understand who and what has shaped your perspective, and the people who work with and for you each have their own backgrounds and points of view. What's important for us as their manager is to understand that point of view. However, research shows that as we rise in an organization and gain power, we often put less effort into understanding other people's perspectives and lose empathy, which makes us less likely to comprehend how others are thinking and feeling, and lowers our ability to adapt our behaviors to accommodate them.[4] As UC Berkeley professor Dacher Keltner explains, "When we don't have power and we want to contribute, we really think carefully about other people, we listen and we adapt our behavior to the social group. But once we have power, our focus shifts to 'What do I want?'"[5] Because of this phenomenon, we may have to work harder at understanding the perspective of those who report to us. This begins with a sincere desire to comprehend that person's viewpoint, recognizing that their perspective is their truth and may differ from our perspective and our truth.

We do not have to agree with their perspective, just to understand it. We can ask open-ended questions to better appreciate how their perspective and their thinking differ from ours. For example, you may ask:

- What do you think is at the root of the problem?

- Could you tell me more about . . . ?
- What do you think would be a good option in this situation?
- What led you to that conclusion?
- Why do you think that is?

When they answer, actively listen to understand the thoughts and emotions behind what they say, what Mark Goulston and John Ullmen discuss in *Real Influence* as connected listening, or listening to fully understand.[6] This involves listening with the intention to truly understand the other person—not only listening to what they're saying, but listening without judgment for how they think and feel about the topic, allowing them time and space to fully express their thinking. It's listening to understand rather than to respond or convince. It may also involve listening to what is not being said, and probing more deeply to understand their perspective.

Megan, the head of sales for a training and development company, stops by all her direct reports' offices on Monday to check in, ask how their weekend was, and inquire about their week ahead. After they tell her, and if she senses that an employee isn't telling her the whole story, Megan gently probes with the question "What else?" to see what else is on their mind or what they're concerned about in the work ahead, and then waits patiently for their response. Through her questions, Megan uncovers what may be worrying her staff so that she can help either in direct assistance or finding the right person to help, protect them from backlash, or simply allay their fears: "But I can only provide this help if I know what's going on."

How We Will Work Together

Because so many people are motivated by purpose, it helps us engage them when we connect their work to the broader mission and purpose of the organization. A good example of this comes from Disneyland, when a family approached a janitor to ask where the Disney Grand Parade would begin. Instead of pointing the way or giving them instructions for how to get there, the janitor picked up his broom, twirled it around, and said, "Follow me!" He then pumped the broom like a drum major's mace, marking time and setting the marching speed, and led the smiling family, including kids dancing along behind him, to the start of the parade. This man understood Disney's vision of creating magical memories for everyone who enters the park.

One of the ways we can most help people and teams perform better is by being clear about our expectations and having "rules for the road" in terms of how we'll work together. One of the practices I've used is having a Team Charter or, as Beat Buhlmann, an interim CIO in Switzerland, calls his, a Communications Driver's License: "When you want to drive, driving is not complicated. But you need to know the rules of the road. Do you drive on the right- or left-hand side of the road? Does a red light mean stop or go? In order to drive in most countries, you need a driver's license, which certifies that you know how to drive and you know the rules of the road. In the US, you drive on the right-hand side of the road, stop at red lights and go on green lights, pass on the left, and pull over if an emergency vehicle behind you has their flashing lights on. That's what makes everyone able to drive there—you all know the rules of the road."

A Team Charter can include the mission of the company and group, roles and responsibilities, norms for meeting times and promptness, and expectations and norms for communication and behaviors. For example, will meetings always start at the appointed time even if key members are running late? How will the team make decisions? How will the team resolve conflict? What channels will the team use to communicate? What is the expected response time? Is it OK to bcc (blind copy) someone on an email? During a meeting, is doing other work or emailing or texting others acceptable? Is yelling a behavior we tolerate? Is everyone expected to contribute to the meeting discussion and, if so, how?

Beat told me about an interesting norm used with one of his teams: Everyone would read any reports or other materials before the meeting and then use the meeting time to discuss those materials. If it became clear during the meeting that someone hadn't done the reading, the meeting would be canceled on the spot. When I asked him if they had ever used that rule, Beat said, "Only once, and the infraction never happened again." And this is an important point about Team Charters: They are not a wish list of desired behaviors; they are the rules of the road that people in the group will adhere to and be held accountable for.

You can also have people create an Operating Manual, or User Manual, to help everyone in the group understand how to work more effectively with one another. When we buy a toaster, it comes with an operating manual to help us understand how to use the toaster effectively and keep it in good working order. An Operating Manual for individuals is similar—it helps us understand how to work well with someone by understanding their style and preferences. For example, in one group I worked with, one of the team members told us that we'll know when he's really stressed out because he'll start cleaning to alleviate that stress. So one day when we came into the office and found him cleaning up the supply closet, we understood what was going on and tried not to add to his stress. Operating Instructions can include many of the elements of the Zig-Zag chart as well as the answers to questions such as these:

- On a regular day, you'll find me to be . . . ?
- What might surprise you about me is . . . ?
- My key strengths include . . . ?
- Some areas of development I'm working on are . . . ?
- What gets me really excited is . . . ?
- My key values are . . . ?
- What some people sometimes misunderstand about me is . . . ?
- What really irritates me is . . . ?

- How I like to be communicated with is . . . ?
- Some traits and qualities I value in other people I work with include . . . ?
- How you'll know that I am feeling stressed or overwhelmed—my "tells" are . . . ?
- The ways I like to relax and unwind include . . . ?
- Other things you should know about me include . . . ?

Feedback: Helping Them Grow/ We Are All a Work in Progress

Feedback is about helping people get better, elevating their skills to increase their abilities, which not only helps them in their career but also helps the team in terms of better collective performance and the organization in terms of results. Just as we need to understand ourselves and then manage ourselves to

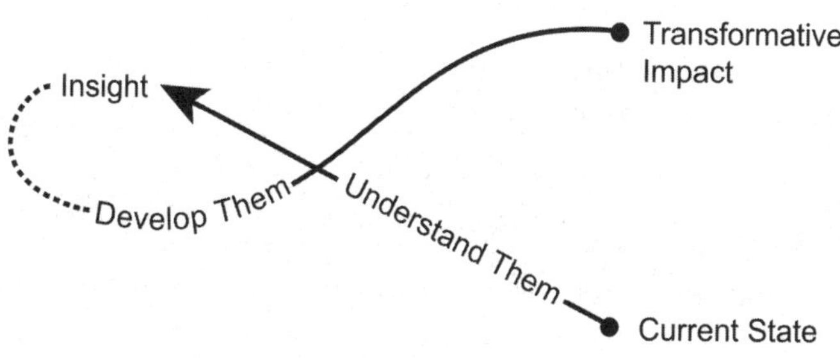

Figure 5.2. The Leading Others Model

our next level, to help others grow we need to not only understand them but also help them develop. And a big part of this is giving them feedback (Figure 5.2).

We are all a work in progress, and development is a process, not an event. To be effective, feedback needs to be "normal," meaning that it is regular and ongoing as well as helpful. This means that it is given in the spirit of development, intended to help people become more effective, rather than to judge or punish them. When I worked in strategy consulting, the firm took the idea of "people are our most valuable assets" seriously and had a strong development culture. This is where Bob told me I needed to speak up more in meetings and bore with me as I made all sorts of embarrassing mistakes along the way to mastering that skill. At this firm, leaders would routinely give feedback, both on what you were doing well, to reinforce that behavior, as well as what behaviors and skills would help us improve our performance. It was a feedback culture where you were expected to grow—and they supported you in doing so. This is quite the opposite of organizations many of us have been in, where when someone told you they wanted to give you some feedback, it seemed to mean "prepare for criticism" and may not have been delivered in either a kind or a developmental manner. It doesn't have to be that way.

Providing timely, constructive feedback is an important practice in developing others, and most of us could get better at formulating and delivering feedback. There are six steps to helping people grow through feedback:

1. **Set your intention(s).** Begin the feedback process by understanding your intentions for giving the feedback. What is it that you want to accomplish in giving feedback to this individual? What behaviors would you like to reinforce or change? How do you want them to think about and act on the feedback they will receive? How do you want them to feel during the interaction? What emotions or behaviors might come up during the feedback session, for either you or the person you're giving feedback to, and how would you like to respond if and when they do?
2. **Formulate what you will say.** Be deliberate in what you will say—the words you choose and the tone you'll adopt—to ensure that the feedback will achieve your intentions. Focus on the behavior of theirs you want to address, whether it is a behavior that is helping them or the team, which is behavior that you want to acknowledge and reinforce, or behavior that is hurting them or the team professionally, which you want to alert them about and help them address. What is the behavior? In what situation(s) have you observed this behavior? And what has been the impact of that behavior? Make it clear that you are asking them to change their behavior, not their personality, and that you want them to succeed and are giving this feedback to enable their development and success.

3. **Practice the delivery.** Write down what you will say and then say it out loud to hear how it may come across to someone else in the words and tone of voice you use. The words you formulate and say in your head often don't sound the same way when those words actually come out of your mouth, so it's helpful to say them aloud before going into a feedback session with others. Practicing your delivery has the added benefit of helping you think through potential reactions and how you would like to respond to those reactions. If you suspect that the receiver of the feedback may become defensive or angry, or might dismiss the feedback, you may want to role-play the scenario with a trusted colleague so you are well prepared for the session and feel more confident in delivering the feedback and in harnessing your own emotions and reactions in the meeting.
4. **Deliver the feedback.** Aim to deliver feedback as close to the observed situation as possible so that the situation you bring up is more easily recalled by the other person. Some feedback can be delivered quickly and informally by dropping by their office or phoning them, and some feedback may need to be scheduled for later if, for example, you are not in the same location, if a web conference is required, or if emotions are running high for either you or the person to whom you will be giving feedback. Often, giving

ourselves and others a chance to calm down before a feedback session increases the likelihood of a productive discussion.

5. **Inquire for understanding and acknowledgment.** Once you deliver the feedback, check in with the recipient to make sure that they understand what you're saying, which might include remembering the situation and behavior you've mentioned and pausing to reflect on and understand the impact of that behavior. Once you know that they understand, you can begin to discuss what might be behind the behavior. What were they thinking and feeling at the time? Delving into the root cause of the behavior both helps them understand why they acted in a certain way and sets the stage for beginning to consider alternative behaviors or actions when they find themselves in a similar situation. Sometimes they may recall the situation and behavior and disagree on the impact or justify the behavior. In these instances, you may need to spend more time helping them to understand another person's perspective or the impact their behavior has not just on other people but also on their reputation and therefore their career.
6. **Guide toward improvement.** Once we have delivered the feedback and know that they understand the impact of their behavior, we can begin to guide them toward replacing their current behavioral pattern

> with a more helpful behavior. If, after the feedback session, you see improvement, mention it to them to reinforce the new behavior. Look for progress, and comment on it rather than waiting for perfection. And if you see a recurrence of behavior they are working to change, mention the situation in another feedback session. This helps them become more mindful of their behavior, which aids them in substituting another, more productive behavior or action in future encounters. It also lets them know we are on their side, supporting their change and holding them accountable for their actions.

In addition to giving feedback to people who work for us, we can also give feedback to peers, as Sue Bevan Baggott, an executive adviser, angel investor, and former global innovation leader at Procter & Gamble, did. Sue had just returned to the United States after a long assignment in Europe for P&G. In her new assignment, she was on a cross-functional team with a hard-charging marketing person: "She was very smart, very driven, and very good at her job. She was also chronically, and significantly, late to every meeting." Sue knew she needed to have a tough conversation with her marketing colleague because it irritated her that every time this woman showed up late, and it was beginning to disrupt their relationship and affect everyone on the multifunctional team: "At first, when I told her that it was being disrespectful to everyone on the team when she was late, she just blew up at me." It was a reaction that Sue hadn't anticipated, and she realized she'd have to have a follow-up conversation with her marketing colleague, this time to repair the relationship and to let her know the feedback wasn't about her, but rather how her chronic lateness was negatively affecting the team: "We were trying to help her succeed, and she was impeding our ability to help her by being late all the time. When I was able to convey this to her, that it was about her behavior, rather than her as a person, she was able to hear it, and she began to change her behavior." It also changed their relationship for the better; as Sue told me, "She later invited me to her wedding."

We can be very direct in our feedback while also being kind. Marian Poirier, whom we met in Chapter 4, is a senior executive based in Australia for a global financial services firm. She told me about the enormous impact of giving regular, honest, and objective feedback to people and getting comfortable with the "constructive" side of the feedback, the part that so many people avoid:

> I've always found that the right people recognize and respect the delivery of constructive feedback. It's very hard, and quite uncomfortable at times, to give constructive feedback to senior colleagues or team members yet, if done right, you end up being respected for it. In fact, when I left my last position, my successor wrote to me, "Your ability to deliver at times brutal

feedback and yet do so in a way that was constructive and never jeopardized your relationships was incredible to behold!"

Mentoring and Coaching

Although "mentoring" and "coaching" are often used as synonyms, they are different techniques. In short, mentoring is more about *telling*, and coaching is more about *asking*. Someone who uses mentoring shares their knowledge, experience, and skills with a mentee by offering advice and guidance. Mentors answer questions about how they would respond to a situation and suggest a course of action for a mentee. Someone who uses coaching does not give advice but rather uses guiding questions to help the person being coached think through a situation, potential courses of actions, and the possible consequences or results of those different actions. The result is that the person being coached develops their own solution to the problem they're facing.

For example, if you mentor someone who is dealing with a difficult situation, you might give them advice on how to interpret the situation, explain how to think about others' perspectives, or suggest things for them to say or do to help resolve the problem. If you were to coach, you might use questions such as "How might you approach this situation?," "How do you think the other person may think or feel about it?," "If you were to use that approach, what might you envision the outcome of that conversation to be?," and "Looking at the situation in this way, what action do you think would be most helpful in resolving it?" Using questions but not providing answers or suggestions allows the person being coached to think through the issue and ultimately choose their own approach, which often increases the likelihood that they will follow through.

With either coaching or mentoring, there may also be times when you want to share instances when you also had to develop as a leader. This may mean sharing some feedback you received in the past and how you addressed the feedback and grew professionally as a result. This shows them that we are human too, which helps us build trust. Recent research found that when leaders display some level of vulnerability, employees are 5.3 times more likely to trust them, and when leaders genuinely acknowledge their failures or shortcomings, employees were 7.5 times more likely to trust these leaders over those who did not.[7]

Dealing with Problem Employees

What constitutes a "problem employee"? A problem employee is someone who is not performing well or is causing difficulties on the team because of their attitude, actions, or behaviors. This can include people who lack motivation or effort, those who are uncooperative on a team, those who are unresponsive to feedback, those who are constant complainers or critics, people who must always prove themselves right, the employee who has a strong opinion about everything and is forceful about sharing that opinion regardless of the circumstances, someone who is ultracompetitive and lacks the collaboration gene, the go-getter who is ambitious beyond their abilities, or people who are rude, abrasive, or passive-aggressive. Although many of these behaviors ultimately result in that person's poor performance, they almost always result in poor team functioning. Either way, when we have a problem employee, we need to take action.

The first action is to look in the mirror. Is there something you are doing that is contributing to the difficult behavior or situation? For example, do we shy away from difficult conversations with the problem employee? Have we perhaps seen this behavior before but not mentioned it because we were uncomfortable giving feedback? Have we not held them accountable for their work quality?

Many years ago, I was taking over a group, and the departing manager came by my office and dropped a large stack of files on my desk, explaining that they were the personnel files for each member of the group I would now be managing, including annual performance reviews. As she got up to leave, the departing manager told me, "I owe you an apology. I should have fired Olivia a long time ago." So, of course, right after she left my office, I opened Olivia's file and looked through her performance reviews. What I saw surprised me—fifteen years of perfect performance reviews. On a one-to-five scale, Olivia received a five out of five for each category each year. In addition, there wasn't a single negative comment in any of the reviews. Having been in the job for only about a week, it was already clear to me that Olivia was not performing well and that the team was suffering because of her lack of performance. Allowing someone to underperform for so many years and drag the overall team's performance and morale down with her was a dereliction of the previous manager's duty. It was also terribly unfair to Olivia, who never had the honest feedback and support that might have helped her become more successful. Giving developmental feedback to our employees is part of our job even if it may surprise or sting the recipient in the short term and may be an uncomfortable conversation for us as well. However, when done well, feedback benefits the recipient and often benefits others in the organization.

Very frequently, people we work with have a different style or come from a different generation, industry, or part of the world where they do things differently than us. Different doesn't necessarily mean difficult—it means different. And in some situations it might be we who are behaving in a difficult manner by avoiding the situation or by not stepping up to give them the developmental feedback that will help them be more successful.

And sometimes we need to give people feedback because they are behaving badly. When this is the case, it may be helpful to remember that people behaving badly are often people in distress and that their poor behaviors are an indication of their being overwhelmed and their inability to cope. Although this doesn't excuse the behavior, it can give us insight into what's behind it. Sometimes we can help these people address the root cause of their distress, and sometimes we cannot. Ultimately, we cannot change their behavior because only *they* can change their behavior. But if this behavior is negatively affecting others, it's our job to address it. This is usually done through feedback about the behavior and its impact on others. And with people who do not listen well or respond well to feedback, we may need to have repeated conversations, including giving them feedback on how they receive or don't receive feedback and how this may affect their career. If people cannot listen to or respond well to developmental feedback, it may be time for a different conversation, one in which you explain the consequences for their behaviors, including the possibility of demotion or termination if they cannot or will not improve. As Beat, the Switzerland-based management consultant and interim manager, told me,

> If someone isn't performing well and is . . . uninterested in putting in the effort to improve, we need to take action. And the longer we wait, the larger the toll this person takes in terms of burning your energy and reputation as a leader. It's also a bad signal to other people on the team who do the hard work, acquire new skills, and perform well. I had a situation like this once before where a person wasn't working out. I called him the chief excuses officer because he had an excuse for why he missed the deadline, why he

was late for the meeting, why he didn't call the client, why the spreadsheet didn't compute. He had an excuse for everything. And I trusted this person too long because, by default, I tend to look for and see the good things in a person, their potential. But it cost me, in terms of trust with the rest of the team. So I haven't made that mistake ever again. When there is a problem person on the team that is not responding to the help you give them, you really do need to take action.

Having Those More Difficult Discussions

One of the more difficult actions we may need to take as a leader is removing someone from our team or separating them from working at the organization. Often called "necessary evils," these are instances when we may cause emotional distress to someone in the service of advancing some larger goal, purpose, or good.[8] For example, we may need to lay someone off during an economic downturn to help the overall company survive, demote or counsel an underperforming employee out of the organization, change someone's role after a restructuring, let someone go when we close an office or plant, or fire a harassing, bullying, or unethical employee for the overall health of the team or company.

These conversations can bring up a mix of emotions for the person on the receiving end as well as for ourselves, including sympathy, anxiety, sadness, guilt, and anger. According to researchers, understanding ourselves and the "emotional cocktail" you are likely to experience when letting someone go is one of the most important parts of doing this painful act well.[9] As with any act of leadership, separations can be done well or poorly.

Having to let someone go, whether it's for simple economics, poor performance, or harmful behavior, is rarely a pleasant experience. I still remember the first time I had to fire someone for poor performance, an action that was particularly difficult because I had hired this employee and liked them very much as a person. However, they were not performing well in their job, and many months of coaching had failed to improve their performance, so I came to the conclusion that I would need to replace them. The organization where I worked had a process for this that included writing a letter to the person. You would hand them this letter at the end of the meeting where you let them know they were being let go, essentially reiterating that they were being separated from the organization and that they would no longer have access to company email, information, or offices. When I showed the letter to the company attorney, he told me that it was the nicest letter he'd ever seen written for a situation like this. "Good," I told him. "That was my intent. I don't believe one needs to be robotic or overly legalistic about these things. I think we need to be human."

The entire week leading up to the separation discussion, I was very anxious about the discussion, and the night before our meeting I barely slept at all. The meeting went as well as a meeting like that could go, but I still felt bad afterward. When

I spoke to my boss about it, I told him that I felt sad about the situation and asked him, a person who had surely had this type of discussion multiple times in his life, if it ever got better. "No," he told me. "It never gets better. And it shouldn't get better. In fact, if letting someone go ever gets easy for you, there's something wrong with you because what you're doing, even if it's warranted, will cause pain to another person. And if you are causing pain for someone else, that should also give you some amount of emotional pain as well." Although a discussion like this may cause pain for someone else, we sometimes have to have these conversations. Sometimes, necessary evils are necessary.

What Can Get in the Way of Leading and Developing Others

Leadership is an inherently human-focused endeavor. As you rise in your career, dealing with people becomes a larger component of your job. The human focus encompasses everything from hiring, developing, and leading individuals, teams, and units to creating the policies that govern these practices for others in the firm. As Phil, the data scientist you met in Chapter 3, told me, "When I contacted someone I worked with that was promoted to CFO about six months after the promotion, he told me he was shocked by how much of his job involved working through people problems: 'I wanted to become CFO because I enjoy finance and figuring out how we can fund growth and maintain financial health. But now, about 50 percent of my job is dealing with people issues.'"

Not everyone is comfortable with or good at developing others, and there are several common reasons for this, including the following:

- **Not understanding that the job of leadership involves leading people.** The job of leadership is about moving people, and organizations filled with these people, toward a different future. And not everyone understands or enjoys this. But because we are leaders, it is part of our job. I've known several people who, as they moved into higher levels of leadership, decided they didn't like managing other people and took a different role. One such person discovered he liked doing the work, rather than leading people, and he left a position where he managed hundreds of people for a high-level advisory role where he's much happier. Whether we like leading and developing others goes back to self-understanding.
- **The knowing-doing gap.** As with managing ourselves, leading others can also involve a knowing-doing gap. Leading other people, in all their complexity, is a difficult task, and often we stop short of applying or putting into practice what we know we should be doing. I once worked alongside someone who was an "expert" on management—they keynoted, consulted, and wrote books on the topic, yet they were not able to put what they knew into practice. They

wrote and taught about treating people with respect, giving credit to those who did the work, giving people the benefit of the doubt, and modeling the desired behavior, but although they knew a lot about leadership, they were not able to do what they knew. Many of us may have been guilty of this at some point in our career. The important thing is self-assessing whether we're actually doing what we know will improve our leadership effectiveness and then going through the messy process of self-managing toward the desired behaviors. In leadership, you don't get credit for knowing how to lead; you get credit for doing it.

- **Poor modeling.** A related concept to the knowing-doing gap is not modeling the behaviors we are working to develop in others. For example, if we are prone to angry outbursts or treating others poorly, we don't have the credibility to ask others to maintain their composure or treat others with respect because we haven't been able to model these behaviors ourselves.
- **Fear of conflict.** Many people fear that a feedback session may turn into a difficult conversation and therefore don't offer the feedback because of their own discomfort during the discussion. So rather than working through their discomfort to have those feedback conversations, they don't have them, hoping

the undesirable behavior will go away or that the other person will figure it out on their own. This was the case when Olivia's boss didn't give her feedback for fifteen years—that manager avoided potentially difficult discussions and therefore didn't give Olivia the developmental feedback she deserved.

- **Being overwhelmed.** Sometimes we are overwhelmed with our own job, and we think that we can't take the time to develop others. In this case, it may be helpful to remember that developing others helps us too. As people evolve in their jobs, their growth benefits us so that we can delegate and turn our focus to more strategic matters.
- **Our own insecurity.** We may fear that developing others will threaten our expertise, stature, or position in the hierarchy or that, once our employees become more proficient, they may compete with us or even outshine us. But we are judged as effective leaders partly on how well our team, and the individuals on our team, perform and grow. In addition, if we don't develop others to the point where they can take on our role, it may inhibit our own career progression.

We Are Modeling All the Time

Leading others is a long-term game, one where we can't know the full extent of our impact on other people as we go along—we can see the cumulative effects only many years later, as in the case of Ashley, who recently retired from the London office of an international management consulting firm. She was surprised to find how many people she had unknowingly influenced throughout her career: "When I was younger in my career, I didn't have a lot of female role models, so it was such a surprise to have so many women, and more than a few men, come up to me and tell me how they learned so much from me and saw me as a role model. I was just doing what I do, and it was so nice to realize that I was also, inadvertently, helping others. The number of people that came up to me, who emailed me, who sent me a letter, who called me was unbelievable, and knowing that I had such a positive impact on so many people is one of the things I'm most proud of in my life."

We measure our leadership by our impact on individuals, organizations, and even societies. Leadership isn't a title or position; it's an attitude and a set of skills and behaviors that can move individuals and organizations forward toward a better future.

6

Managing Up

"A promotion I had a few years ago was a double-edge sword," John, the CFO of a large health-care company, told me. The promotion came with a nice increase in compensation, more responsibility, and a company car. But there was also a downside—John would now report to the CFO, Nathan, who had a reputation for being very difficult to work with: "Like a lot of really smart people, Nathan was impatient with people that couldn't keep up with his quick thinking or didn't understand his vision. He was blunt, rude, and led like a dictator—through intimidation and fear. He was a real bully." And although turnover on Nathan's team was very high, the company looked the other way because he produced results.

"I often think that people like Nathan are insecure and using a tough exterior to hide that insecurity. So what they need is to feel like they are in charge and that others are working to help them, not against them," John told me. "I spent many years in consulting and tend to think of my boss as another client whose problems I'm helping to solve, and that's how I approached my relationship with Nathan." Rather than just accepting and executing all of Nathan's direct orders, John helped him think through problems and solutions, helped him come up with innovative ideas, and kept him apprised of what was going on further down in the team and in other parts of the organization.

"I have a positive attitude and am relatively easy to get along with, but it took a lot to get through to Nathan," John told me. "I tried very hard to make a connection with him, so in every interaction I'd slip in a bit of humanity, let him know something about me, ask him a question about himself, ask for his advice on something, or tell him about what was going on with the team. I wanted him to see me as a person, not just an extra set of hands. I wanted him to know that there was a brain, and goodwill, that went with that extra set of hands."

After several months, Nathan began to realize that John was intelligent, insightful, discreet, and helpful, and he began to warm up. "For example," John told me, "people used to give Nathan the quarterly financials for the earnings call, and Nathan would take it from there. I'm good at helping people understand the numbers using a narrative, so I helped him explain the story behind the numbers, including what got us to these numbers and where the numbers are trending for the next quarter." Nathan's presentations improved significantly, and John's assistance in making this happen helped build their relationship. As John told me, "I think that's when Nathan realized that I could be a good thought partner for him." The team's results improved, and John began to bring in and highlight the work of others on the team: "Over time, Nathan became more open to input from them too. And while he was still not a great boss, he was a much better one, and it got a lot nicer to work in the finance function."

John's story illustrates successfully working with a difficult manager. If you've ever had a difficult boss, you know how delicate a situation like this can be.

We spent the last chapter discussing how we can grow our employees. In this chapter, we'll focus on how we might approach our relationship with our own manager to improve results, help make them more successful, and help them help us in our career and professional growth.

What Is "Managing Up"?

Our manager is one of the most important stakeholders in our career and professional development. This can be a tricky relationship to negotiate because our boss may have more experience than we do, have access to different information and networks than we do, and be at a higher level in the hierarchy, meaning that there is also a power differential to manage as part of the relationship.

Managing up is taking responsibility for the relationship with your manager. Because of their place in the organizational hierarchy and the asymmetry of power that this entails, managing your boss takes care, planning, and tact. Because our managers have a lot of power in our career, managing up is a proactive strategy for managing our career. Our manager can be a source for advice and guidance, as well as a sponsor for our career, so not managing up may ensure that we don't get these benefits.

Just as the employees we lead are unique, so too are the people who are charged with leading us. And just as there is no single right way to lead employees, the same is true of managing up. Our boss is a unique individual who deserves respect and support, just as our employees do and just as we do. With our boss, we have a mutually dependent relationship in which we both rely on, and have expectations for, the other. Our boss also has a lot of relationships to manage, and it's likely that their relationship with us may not be their most important relationship to manage. It's also likely that advancing our career is not their top priority.

How to Manage Up

Managing up is about helping your boss succeed, supporting their work, and complementing their style. Although you don't need to be exactly like your boss to succeed at having a relationship with them, understanding them can help you follow their lead and help them deliver better results. There are several key aspects of managing up:

- **Understand your boss.** The more we understand about our manager's job—what they're on the hook for; what their salary, bonus, or promotion depends on; what pressures they're under; what priorities they're juggling—the more we can anticipate their needs and concerns, and the more we can help them. Perhaps your manager has a difficult boss. They might be responsible for a project or product line that is not doing well. Or they may be managing a difficult situation in their personal life (e.g., divorce or illness in the family) that leaves them distracted at work. What are their strengths and weaknesses? What are their goals and priorities? What problems and pressures are they facing? How might you help them? Who and what has shaped their worldview? What is their background and experience, and how might these factors have influenced them and the way they lead? What values do they exhibit or discuss? How do they like to be communicated with? What is their style? Just as each of your employees is different, your boss has their own idiosyncrasies. Using a Zig-Zag chart (see Chapter 5) can also be helpful in understanding how and where you and your boss are similar or different in style and in your approach to problems.

- **Think like a partner.** If we think of our boss like a partner, it changes the way we approach the relationship. When we think like a partner, as John did with Nathan, we do what we can to help them be successful. We think win-win. We discuss issues with them, assuming positive intent on their side. We give them the benefit of the doubt. We speak well of them when they're not around. We care about their well-being, both personally and professionally. Are there areas in which you might think more like a partner with your manager?

- **Demonstrate your value.** Above all, do your job well. Being reliably good at your job gives you credibility and affords you a level of autonomy because your boss can turn their attention elsewhere. To what extent does your boss believe that you do your job well? What might you do to improve in this area—either in doing your job well or helping your boss understand that you have it under control?

Even with understanding our boss, thinking like a partner, and demonstrating our value, we may not be able to "break through" and have a solid, trusting, mutually supportive relationship with our manager, and often the signs are there from the beginning of the relationship, as organizational psychologist and coach Gena Cox discovered: "Several years ago, I was working on a remote team and noticed one day that everyone on the call had an orchid on their desk. I asked why everyone had an orchid, and they told me that the orchids were for Mother's Day. Their boss had given each of them an orchid to celebrate." Gena was a mother too, and had the same orchid-giving boss as the others on the web meeting but wasn't sent an orchid. When she met with her boss a few days later, she asked him why she didn't get an orchid. "He told me, 'Gosh, I didn't send you an orchid because I didn't know you were a mother.' I realized how strange it was that he didn't know the one thing about me that I valued most. And it made me wonder why he didn't know this because it was something most people knew about me. Then I remembered the first day we met, when he kept me waiting in the lobby for forty-five minutes before he came out to interview me. And he never acknowledged the delay or apologized about it. I felt he had no genuine interest in me as a person. I felt disrespected from Day One." And that type of behavior continued: "The orchid incident helped me realize that he was never going to take an interest in me or my career. It was very clear that I didn't matter to him, and I began to ask myself why I was even there. I left shortly after that. It was such a great reminder to me that, when you're a leader, you need to think about your behaviors from the perspective of those you lead; if people you lead perceive that they are not important to you, there is a high risk they will leave your team. Being too busy to attend to how others perceive you is a luxury leaders cannot afford."

Transitions

Transitioning from one manager to another can be a stressful situation. Whether the transition occurs because of a reorganization, a peer being promoted to manage the team, or our current manager taking a position at another company, being promoted to another position within the current company, retiring, or being fired, the scenario offers both potential peril and opportunity. Research shows that transitions, including having a new manager, can be tricky and, if not managed well, can lead to a career slowdown and even a derailment.[1] And as we saw with how John approached Nathan and will see with some other examples below, these transitions can be managed quite successfully. You're starting over with this new manager and will need to get to know, support, and build a relationship with this new boss.

Having a manager you've worked with for many years leave and a new one take over can be a difficult situation, particularly if you had a successful relationship with the previous manager. It can be frustrating and nerve-racking at times because you get no credit for the work you did in the past or the great relationship you established with your previous boss. Although the new manager may have goals similar to those of the previous one, the new manager is likely to have a very different style. Here are a few questions I've used that can help you better understand a new manager:

- How can I help you get acclimated to the company/team/clients?

- What short-term goals and priorities do you have that I might support you in achieving?

- What's the one thing I can do in my position to most help you in yours?

- What might I do that would inadvertently annoy you?

- What is the best way for me to communicate with you? Do you have a preferred channel for communication, and do you have expectations for what and how often I should communicate with you?

These questions can help us better understand our new boss, how they like to work, what types of behaviors they value, and how we can be intentional in working with them and meeting their expectations. You can also ask them some of the User Manual questions from Chapter 5 and share your own answers to these questions to help them get to know you. In addition, if our new boss comes from within the organization, we can talk to people they have previously worked with to better understand them.

Abrupt transitions, such as when your boss is fired, can spell opportunity and turbocharge your career if you communicate effectively and advocate for yourself with higher-ups, as Alexandra, a Europe-based senior executive in a global financial services firm, found. When Alexandra's boss was let go, it turned out to be the biggest turning point in her career. At the time, she was head of relationship management for the entire Americas region, and her boss, a managing director, had responsibility for both relationship management and sales. It was a big job. "When he was let go," Alexandra said, "the firm tapped me to replace him, but gave the sales piece to someone else. So it really didn't feel like they were giving me his job." Alexandra made the case to her boss's boss that she had already been doing her manager's job, except for the sales-management piece, and was ready for the bigger job with both the sales- and relationship-management components. "This is a very sales-driven organization, and there's a sense that if you haven't come from the sales side, you can't *possibly* understand what it's like to do sales and therefore can't lead a sales team. Clearly, I wasn't the obvious choice, but I told them they would be hiring me into the job as a business manager, not just a sales manager. My reasoning prevailed, and I was ultimately, and somewhat reluctantly, given the job."

It was a difficult transition for Alexandra at first because she was the first nonsalesperson to run the unit, and it took some time to gain the trust of the sales team:

> As a business leader, I focused on the business issues and supporting the sales team, which helped me gain

their trust. And guess what? Sales increased, and the unit was quite successful, and, based on this work, I was promoted to managing director for the European division and then, a few years later, became head of the entire international business. But it all started when I stepped up and said, "I can do this!" when I wasn't the obvious choice, and then doing that job well. I seriously doubt I would have ended up as head of the European division had I not done that.

Sometimes, a poorly performing boss or a reorganization can create an awkward scenario, as happened to Megan, head of sales for a training and development company. "At one point in my career, I worked in sales for someone that was a really nice person, but not an effective sales manager," Megan told me. "She would get very flustered any time there was pressure, and in sales there is always a lot of pressure." After a few years, the company switched their roles, and Megan was not only being promoted above the people who had been her peers, but her boss was demoted, and Megan would now be her boss: "It was pretty awkward at first because she was a lot older than I was and not only had she been my boss for years, but we were friendly, and the relationship dynamics changed quite a bit." There was a lot of talk about the situation throughout the office, and as Megan told me, "I figured she felt awkward about the situation too, so I needed to address it head-on." Once the decision had been made, Megan went to talk with her. "I said,

'Look, we just need to talk about this openly because I would feel really awkward if all of a sudden I took the job and didn't have this direct conversation with you,' and I think she appreciated this. We both acknowledged the awkwardness of the situation and vowed to work through it together." And they did.

Whatever the situation we have with a new manager—or with our previous manager becoming our employee—it takes care and tact to finesse the situation and build rapport.

A Note on Truly Terrible, Horrible, No-Good, Very Bad Bosses

Most of us will work for a really bad boss at some point in our lives, perhaps more than one. Research by the Harris Poll bears this out, showing that more than 70 percent of workers have had at least one such noxious manager in their career.[2] These difficult managers can range from inexperienced and incompetent bosses to truly mean-spirited individuals who have little regard for human suffering. Researchers have found that when we experience incivility in the workplace, about half of people intentionally decreased their work effort, more than three-quarters said it decreased their commitment to the organization involved, and more than one in ten said they had left a job because of poor treatment/behavior.[3]

We have a lot of discussion about "bad bosses" in MYLO, and what's interesting is that many people come in thinking "It's all their [the bosses'] fault" when, in fact, we often play a role in the difficult relationship. Just as we discussed when working with a problem employee, when we have a less-than-ideal boss, it's also helpful to look in the mirror, for there may be some things we are doing that contribute to the situation. In addition, it's easy to mistake incompetence for ill intent toward us. Keeping this in mind may give us a bit more empathy for a previous bad boss because we learn our own leadership skills by leading others, just as that previous bad boss had to learn to lead by leading us.

Sometimes we learn how to manage up by having a very difficult manager. Sofia, a software sales executive, told a story in one of my professional development classes that created a lot of discussion and reflection from others about their own situation: "When I was in my thirties, I had a really difficult boss that made my life miserable for several years. In the beginning, he mostly ignored me, and the more successful I became, the worse his behavior toward me became." The company, a software firm, had been losing customers and was in a financial dip when Sofia joined, so the first thing she did as a new sales rep was to start calling customers to get to know them, ask questions about their experience with the company's software and service, and see how she might better understand what they needed. During those calls, Sofia found a lot of interesting information that allowed her to build strong relationships with these customers. It also helped her make a lot of money for the company.

"I wrote up my interview findings and sent the document around to others in the local office," Sofia told me. "And those people sent it out to the international sales team and to people in the product-development team. Suddenly, I was on the map within the company, and people knew who I was. However, this new notoriety made the situation with my boss worse. At this point, he went from ignoring me to being overtly negative and mildly hostile. But I kept my head down and kept plugging away. Every day felt like a battle to stay focused on the job at hand while my boss, someone who was supposed to support me, actively worked against me."

Within two years, Sofia became the top salesperson in the firm and began negotiating some very big contracts. Soon thereafter she negotiated the biggest contract in the firm's history: "It took 250 meetings over a full year to land that contract. And it was a very big deal for the company. What my boss did next shocked me—he sent out a firm-wide announcement about the new contract, and the announcement didn't even mention my name. It said the deal came to fruition through his work, although he'd had very little involvement in the deal, and that of another person, someone who had joined the firm the previous month and was not involved in the deal *at all.* That was my final straw and was the first and only time I ever quit a job on the spot, without having another job in hand."

Before starting her next job, Sofia reflected on what happened and realized that she had contributed to making a bad situation worse. Although her boss had been a terrible manager, she had never stood up to him and told him that what he was doing was not just graceless and demotivating but harmful as well. From this reflection, Sofia vowed to never again put up with bad behavior from her boss or anyone else she worked with:

> This decision was tested early in my next job. When a senior manager sent an email to me, copying others, with some derogatory comments about people from my region of the world, I went to talk with him about it. He seemed surprised that I would bring it up and then became defensive, telling me that it was just a joke. But I told him it wasn't a joke—it was rude, inappropriate behavior and not funny in any way. The meeting was tense, and I don't think I changed his mind, but he knew I wouldn't stand for that type of behavior, and it has never happened again.
>
> These experiences taught me the importance of stepping up and standing out in my career. Rather than working so hard to fit in, I became more of myself. I stopped being so quiet and started speaking up, asking more questions and offering my own opinions. It made a huge difference in the way I operated and the way people perceived me. I would not be in the position I'm in today, leading the entire sales team, if I'd continued to try to blend in like the quiet, dutiful young woman I'd been.

Hallmarks of some truly terrible managers include those who are absent or incommunicado, unavailable for advice and guidance when you most need it, and those who have a need for control and exhibit domineering behavior, such as interrupting, talking over, criticizing, bullying, throwing tantrums, humiliating others in public, and other behaviors that make people fearful. It can include those who are threatened by our skills or success and micromanage us to prove their worth; limit our access to certain information, conversations, or people; criticize or belittle us to "put us in our place"; or treat us with some of the above domineering behaviors to undermine our confidence. It can also include bosses who overpromise and don't deliver on their promises (e.g., for promotions or for less overwork). Some of these managers surround themselves with "yes people" and mediocre talent to make themselves feel smart and powerful. Really bad bosses can be soul-crushing and draining to work with.

Regarding regulating our own behaviors in working with people who are behaving badly, Thich Nhat Hanh has an interesting perspective: "When another person makes you suffer, it is because he suffers deeply within himself, and his suffering is spilling over."[4] It helps us realize that when a boss, or any other person, treats us badly, their behavior may have very little to do with us and more to do with what is going on in their own world. But although we cannot control how others think or behave, we do have control over ourselves and our behavior.

When you have an insecure boss, there are some things you can do to make the situation more palatable. First, let them know, and feel, that they are in charge. Don't challenge them, particularly in front of others. Keep track of your own contributions and successes so they will be top of mind when they tell you that you have not made any contributions. And learn as much as you can from them while you're there and network widely to expand your learning, contacts, and opportunities. Sometimes the biggest learning from these situations is that you never want to make anyone feel the way this boss makes you feel. That's still a valuable lesson.

We can learn from our most difficult bosses, even if it's not pleasant. Daniel Mouen Makoua, a London-based leader of a global environmental services company, told me about a difficult manager he once worked for:

> I had a really demanding boss one time, when I was head of strategy for an investment-management firm and he was the chairman and chief executive of the company. I learned that to meet his expectations when given a task I had to be extremely comprehensive in the work that I was handing back and think three or four steps ahead when preparing my work; this meant answering the direct question, anticipating the next set of questions he would ask, and repeating the process several more times until I got to an answer that was thorough, precise, well substantiated, actionable, cost-effective, and in line with the business strategy. It was challenging to work with him, but I learned a lot about how to really

> consider a question from many different angles and use the answers to various questions to converge on an answer. He was tough, though, and I stayed with him for two years—most other people only lasted for six months with him.

If you work with a difficult person, keep in mind that you cannot change them and their behaviors. Only they can make these changes. However, if you think your difficult boss might want to change—if they understood the negative impact they are having on you and others—it may help to have a conversation about the situation and the impact of their behaviors. If you don't think they would want to change or they wouldn't take the feedback well coming from you, then attempting such a conversation could make your situation worse. And even if they profess a desire or commitment to change, they may or may not understand themselves or have the ability to manage themselves well. Their own self-understanding and ability to self-manage is not up to you or even about you, but it can have a strong impact on you. When you have a really horrible, no-good boss, one that is demeaning or abusive, it may be helpful to remember that their behavior says more about them than it does about you. Although it's never pleasant to have an abusive manager, remembering this may help you to not take their behavior personally. It doesn't excuse their behavior, but it may help you put it in perspective.

You own your behavior; they own theirs. As author and pastor Dave Willis once said, "Show respect even to people that don't deserve it—not as a reflection of their character, but as a reflection of yours."[5] This advice may be helpful in not exacerbating an already difficult problem or avoiding having your behavior become what gets singled out for punishment. But if you continue to work with an abusive manager who diminishes you, it can negatively affect your motivation, confidence, mental health, and career. In these situations, you may want to take the learning and move on.

Should I Stay or Should I Go?

One of the most common questions in my programs is about whether people should stay in their current job with a difficult manager or leave in search of greener pastures. The question arises sometimes because they have a difficult team member or boss, and other times because people feel restless or "stuck" in their current position and are wondering if that's a sign to move on. The answer to this question is, like so many others, "It depends." It depends on what your goals are for your career, for learning, for experience; your appetite for comfort versus adventure; how you think about remuneration and learning; and how uncomfortable your current situation is. There is no promise that the situation you are in will get better, and there's no guarantee that a new job will have a better manager. Many of us have stayed with bad or even very bad bosses longer than we "should have," and we have left other difficult managers whom we might have stayed with longer and learned from.

Just as our boss can fire us, we can fire our boss by leaving them or the organization. Some helpful "should I stay or should I go" questions to help you assess whether it's time to begin looking for another position and manager include these:

- What have I learned from this person, and in this position, so far?
- Is there still an opportunity for me to continue to learn and grow in this position, working for this manager? If so, what is it that I want to learn, and how might I go about obtaining this knowledge and growth?
- To what extent are the skills I'll continue to learn be transferrable to other jobs or careers I may want in the future?
- Do my reasons for considering leaving this manager have to do with ethical lapses in the manager or organization?
- Is working for this person negatively affecting my mental health?
- Are there people higher up in the organization whom I admire or aspire to be like?

Even when your answers to the above questions point to "I should go," there may be times when leaving a bad boss may not be a viable short-term solution. In these situations, it can be helpful to focus on what you can learn while you remain there, which may include taking on new projects or challenges, networking widely within the company, or practicing dealing with a difficult, demanding person. However, working with a bad boss comes with an emotional and sometimes physical toll, and the longer you continue to work with them, the larger the overall toll it will take.

When leaving a bad boss or situation, as hard as it may be, plan to make a graceful exit. Rage quitting, including creating an ugly scene on your way out or leaving a mess for your manager, others on the team, and the person who comes in behind you, may feel satisfying in the moment or even justified based on the way you've been treated, but it's rarely a good option for your long-term reputation. Making a graceful exit means making a transition plan to help the person who comes in behind you understand the relevant processes and know where to find key information, thanking your manager for what you've learned from them, tying up as many loose ends as possible, being constructive in explaining why you're leaving, and offering to answer some questions in the weeks following your departure.

PART THREE

Understanding and Managing Organizational Context

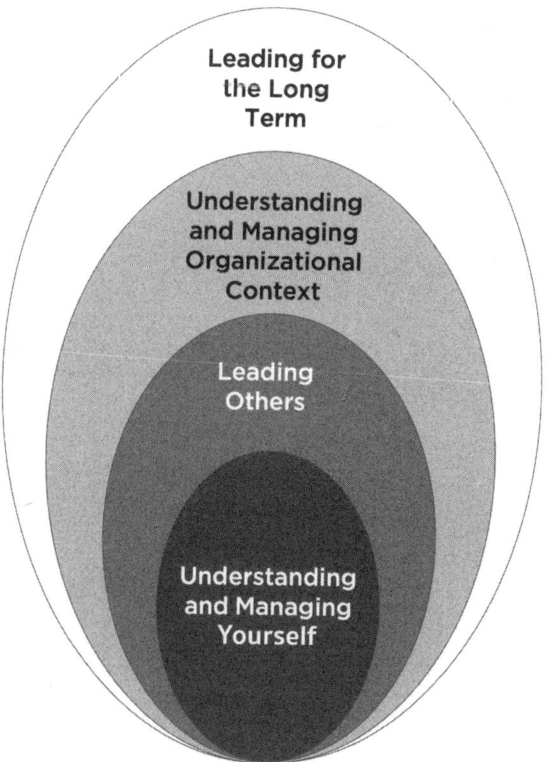

7

Understanding Organizational Culture

Rob Duboff, who cofounded Boston-based research and consulting firm HawkPartners, told me about a previous job he'd had as chief marketing officer for an international accounting and consulting firm: "I'd been a consultant for most of my life, so knew the industry, process, and sales cycle pretty well. But I'd switched sides, and rather than selling and managing the work, my role now was to figure out how to spend our $95 million marketing budget. I also went from a midsize firm to a very large, international firm, and now had 350 people reporting to me." And the culture was quite different: "Because the firm had its roots in accounting, it was more conservative, hierarchical, and political than anywhere I'd ever worked." The firm was almost everything the opposite of Rob:

"I'm extroverted, and the people there, even people in the office next to me, would rather send an email than come into my office to talk about whatever was on their mind. And although I like data and analysis, I also use my gut to make decisions, whereas the firm was not this way. To discuss feelings or what your gut told you in decision-making was anathema there. And I never really picked up on some of those cues until much later."

A year later, the CEO who hired Rob retired, and when the new CEO took over, one of his first moves was to sell off a division. As a result, Rob's marketing budget was cut significantly, and the new CEO told Rob he'd have to lay off a third of his staff. This type of maneuver, a large-scale layoff, went against Rob's values, and he began to look for cost savings to avoid this step. But it was not what his boss had asked for: "I told him that I don't believe in resorting first to a layoff. But the new CEO said, 'I do believe in it.'" That's when Rob realized it was not only his style that clashed with others in the firm but, more importantly, his values. At this point, Rob decided to try another tack to prevent the mass layoffs: He told the CEO that he and two of the other most highly paid staff would resign. As Rob told me, "I thought that was a much better solution to the problem." The amount of money the company saved by not having these three salaries meant the layoff was ultimately much smaller than originally planned, and one of the three who resigned went on to a more satisfying corporate job while Rob and his other colleague started a successful company together, one based on their own values.

When we work in an organization, culture is all around us. It's a strong force in an organization, so it's helpful to understand what it is and how it operates. We may want to change culture, which we'll discuss later in this chapter, and being part of any organizational culture may also change us. Understanding ourselves through the exercises in Chapters 1–3 can also help us understand what type of culture may be a good fit for us. And, while many companies also have subcultures, this chapter will focus on overall organizational culture.

What Is Organizational Culture, and How Can We Understand It?

A 2018 *Harvard Business Review* article summarized the work of leading organizational culture researchers and distilled the idea of culture to focus on norms that reveal and shape the behaviors and thinking of those within the organization: "Culture is the tacit social order of an organization: It shapes attitudes and behaviors in wide-ranging and durable ways. Cultural norms define what is encouraged, discouraged, accepted, or rejected within a group."[1]

At a high level, we often discuss culture as "the way things work" or "the way we do things" at various organizations, and it's unique to each one. Culture has to do with norms and behaviors, with what type of presentation—including behaviors, dress, decoration, and level of individuality—is expected and valued. For example, in some companies angry outbursts and aggressive behavior are the norm, and in others that type of behavior would get you fired. In some organizations everyone looks to the leader for their opinion before taking action, and in others people take action with autonomy. In some firms most of the leaders come from similar backgrounds, or are of the same race or sex, or were educated at a handful of certain schools, and in others leadership is more diverse. In some organizations most people leave work at five or six o'clock and don't check email at night, and in others people work all hours of the day and night.

During my consulting days, I worked with an organization in the beverage industry where to be considered for leadership positions, people had to come from a small list of top schools. Another organization, in financial services, was very specific about dress codes, going to the level of recommending women wear gold jewelry, not silver, because it better fit the image of the firm. This same firm had very little racial or gender diversity in leadership positions, and the entirety of the leadership team came up through the ranks of the sales function. Another client had a clean-desk policy and discouraged people from having any personal items like photos or mementos visible. This is quite different from another client company in the same industry that let each person design their own space, allowing offices and workstations to reflect each employee's personality and what was important to them. As you might imagine, these two firms' offices looked very different and gave off very different vibes.

Although culture doesn't explain everything about how an organization approaches problems or what behaviors are encouraged or discouraged, it can help us interpret what is expected and rewarded there. And although not everyone in the company will be the same or will think or behave in the exact same way, the culture can help explain the general way the organization approaches problems.

Edgar Schein of MIT was among the first to study organizational culture, and according to him, culture can be understood in three distinct layers.[2] The model is often drawn in a pyramid shape, with what is visible at the top and what is invisible, and harder to understand, below that. At the top of the pyramid are the *artifacts* of culture, which are often things that you can see, hear, and feel. For example, artifacts of culture can include the design of facilities and workspaces (e.g., modern or traditional, luxurious or utilitarian), how people dress (e.g., formally or informally, similarly or with more individual style on display), and behavioral norms (e.g., people may use titles in addressing others, such as "Doctor," or address people by their first name or even nicknames; swearing may be common or uncommon; people may talk with colleagues about their life outside work or keep conversations focused on the business of the organization).

Although it's easy to see or feel these artifacts, it can be difficult to understand their meaning. For example, a company that has expensive artwork on the walls may do so because it is proud of its success and is showing what its success can buy, or this may mean that the company believes that fine art puts people at ease or makes them think more creatively. Or an organization that has an old, run-down building may indicate a lack of funds to improve the facilities, or it may indicate an organization that does not prioritize aesthetics and human comfort. Artifacts need interpretation, usually from someone who has been in the organization for a long time.

Below the level of artifacts is the level of *espoused values*—this is what the organization *says* about its culture, its values, and the way it approaches work. We can often see an organization's espoused values on display in the mission and vision statements. We can also understand espoused values from how people explain the artifacts of culture—for example, how they talk about the way people dress or behave in the office, or how they explain the rituals of the organization. Espoused values often come up as the answer to the question a new employee might ask about "Why do we do it this way?" Beyond what you might see in the mission statement, espoused values are often revealed in organizational newsletters and other communication vehicles. Often, the espoused values are more *aspirational* than actual—for example, when an organization publicizes how customer-centric it is yet focuses on sales targets or when an organization talks about work/nonwork balance and employee well-being yet lionizes people who work an extraordinary number of hours (e.g., winning a "Whatever It Takes" award). And then there's Enron, which had integrity as one of its shared values and whose executives perpetrated one of the largest accounting-fraud cases in history.

At the base of the pyramid are what Schein calls *shared tacit assumptions*, the underlying, deeply held beliefs of the people in the company that often come from the organization's founders or leaders during pivotal events in the company's life. These are the true explanations for why people do what they do in a certain way, as well as for what people in the organization value, celebrate, or punish, as well as for what they believe. These are the deeply held beliefs about human nature, what's right and what's wrong, how people work together, and what behaviors will lead to workplace success (or failure) that drive the organization's approach to problems, how it weighs options, and how it evaluates trade-offs.[3]

When an organization's leaders tell you what they believe, these are *espoused* values, and when the leaders make a decision, for example, on whom to promote or whether to implement a new policy, it reveals the organization's *enacted* values, which are the *expression* of its shared tacit assumptions. A classic example of espoused values being different from enacted values is an organization that includes items such as collegiality, cooperation, and diversity in its mission and values statements yet rewards and promotes, and often celebrates, people who are sharp-elbowed, self-centered, or all from a similar background.

With culture, actions speak louder than words: These actions reveal an organization's shared tacit assumptions. It's the old "pay attention to what they do, not what they say" idea. What leaders at an organization do or tolerate—their *enacted* values—is more indicative of their true values, their shared tacit assumptions, than what they say about their values. As Donald Sull of MIT points out, "The sharpest test of whether a corporate culture truly respects employees is how senior leaders deal with managers who hit their numbers but abuse their team."[4]

A company's shared tacit assumptions, those deeply held beliefs, define what to pay attention to, what things mean, and what actions to take in various kinds of situations. These beliefs and values are taken for granted, they are deeply rooted in how the organization works, and people have become socialized into them as they work in that company. And this is why it can be difficult to change an organization's culture. Not impossible, but not easy.

Understanding an organization's culture tells you what is expected, what is tolerated, and what is rewarded in that company and therefore what behaviors and what types of people succeed there.

Culture Begins with the Founder

People have personalities, and organizations have cultures; particularly for small, young companies, the culture of an organization reflects the founder. If you are the founder of an organization, the values you exhibit and the behavior you encourage (or tolerate) will become entrenched in the organization's culture as the firm grows. The original culture of an organization begins with the founder, and the "how we do things around here" can usually be linked back to the personality, preferences, and style of the founder. As Schein says, "It is in the nature of entrepreneurial thinking to have strong ideas about what to do and how to do it. Founders generally have well-articulated theories of their own about how groups should work, and they most often select as colleagues and subordinates people who they sense will think like them."[5] So if the founder was an extraverted person who enjoyed parties, that organization may tend to have a more extraverted, social culture. If the founder was highly competitive and had a win-lose attitude, the organization may foster that environment among employees and have a noncollaborative, and even cutthroat, culture. To truly understand the origins of an organization's culture, it's important to understand the founder. What were they like? What was their background? What drove them to start the company? What did they value? What were some of their assumptions? And how did their way of thinking and working set the tone and approach that became the culture of the organization?

Culture flows from those who started the company and is strengthened as they later hire and promote people with similar values and ways of thinking. People who align with this way of thinking and behaving are attracted to that organization and tend to thrive there. Those who don't align are often repelled by the culture and don't join that organization or, if they do join, may find it a stressful place to work and often don't thrive there. That's how culture becomes deeply embedded in the company and the way people think and behave there. For smaller and younger organizations where the founder is still leading the company or is only a generation or so out of running the company, we can really feel the founder's personal imprint.

Carla, a Chicago-based partner in an international consulting firm, told me about one of her most memorable client engagements: "The firm, an IT services company, had what I'd call a 'firefighting' culture. By this, I mean they valued people that performed well in a crisis, those that would do whatever it took, including working extreme hours and driving others to do the same, to fix whatever crisis that was going on at the time. And it wasn't like the company only had a crisis occasionally. No, this company had crises *all the time*." According to Carla, the company seemed to enjoy having crises just so they could "put out the fire." The founder had spent his early career working in a big bank with a strong hierarchy and very bureaucratic processes, including a cumbersome, deliberative, time-consuming decision-making process that frustrated and confounded him and caused the bank to miss important opportunities because it was just too slow. Railing against that type of culture, this man left the bank and started an IT services company.

"This founder had a bias for action, believed that fast decision-making was important, and chided people who 'overthought' decisions or 'took too long' to make a decision," Carla told me. "He valued fast decision-making and didn't worry much about making the wrong decision, believing that most decisions that proved to be suboptimal could be unwound and then a different decision could be made and implemented. The important thing was making fast decisions." However, the founder seemed to consider only the speed of making the initial decision, not the time spent implementing the decision, realizing it was not a good initial decision, rethinking the problem, and then coming up with a new decision, unwinding the work that had already been done, and implementing the new decision. This way of working led to some very quick but bad decisions made and implemented, many crises when things didn't work as expected, and a lot of wasted effort: "It was heartbreaking because they were burning out, and losing very strong performers, and if they'd spent only a bit longer thinking about the problem and potential solutions, they would have come up with a better solution the first time. What's worse is that people were often rewarded and considered heroes if they resolved the crisis even if they created the crisis themselves due to making a poor decision. It was an organization that valued firefighting and hired arsonists!"

Carla and her team's main recommendation to the company was to slow down and reevaluate its decision-making process to alleviate many of the problems it was experiencing. Although the leadership team agreed with the recommendations, they were ultimately unable to implement them. The quick decision-making and bias for action were so much a part of the way they thought and approached problems that they were ultimately unable to change the way they operated. The company did not go out of business, but employee turnover remained high, and overall performance continued to be lackluster.

Culture Takers and Culture Makers

When thinking about culture, particularly your ability to influence, evolve, or change a culture, it's helpful to think about culture makers and culture takers. The vast majority of people working in an organization, particularly midsize and large organizations, including many of those in very high-level senior management positions, are culture takers, meaning that they join an existing organizational culture and work within that culture. They are expected to adapt to the culture and very quickly learn "how we do things around here." For a culture taker it's important to understand the culture of the organization we work in: It determines our working environment as well as what types of skills and behaviors are expected and rewarded versus discouraged or punished. Because of this, some cultures may be more comfortable for us than others. When you join an organization, culture is socialized, and even though cultural rules and expectations are rarely written down and discussed, there is a social order and ways of thinking that people begin to understand as they work there. And culture is important in leadership because it shapes how people behave and what types of people succeed in that organization, including those who join at non-C-suite senior levels.

People at the very top of an organization—particularly the CEO—are culture makers, and because they control key resources and make policy and procedural decisions, they are the ones who have the power to shape culture. Culture makers have access to, and power over, many of the levers available in managing culture, including organizational structure, organizational strategy, what type of people are recruited into the organization, how work is done, what benefits are offered, what type of learning and development opportunities are available, criteria for rewards and promotions, whether the company allows unethical or abusive behavior, and how the organization responds to crises or downturns.[6] Although culture takers may be able to influence how their individual teams work, the true power to change an organization's culture lies with the senior-most leader of the company. It's not that culture takers are unable to change an organization's culture because they are lazy or incompetent—culture takers cannot change the culture because they are not in a position of power and do not control the levers that could create culture change. Ultimately, the chief executive officer is also the chief cultural officer.

As an employee of an organization, even as a senior leader, you are more often a culture taker than a culture maker. In the opening vignette even Rob, who reported directly to the CEO, was a culture taker. Beyond the C-suite, most of us are culture takers.

Can We Change a Culture?

If you are in the C-suite, you are in a position to change culture, although changing an organizational culture is not an easy or quick process. As Niccolò Machiavelli, an Italian Renaissance historian, politician, and philosopher, wrote in his book *The Prince*, "There is nothing more difficult to take in hand, more perilous to conduct, or more uncertain in its success than to take the lead in the introduction of a new order of things." Although he wrote this several hundred years ago, it's still true.

However, to address upcoming or ongoing market changes or revive an organization in decline, a leadership team sometimes needs to evolve the culture. When technology changes, new discoveries are made, stakeholder needs evolve, markets shift, and regulations change, the strategies that made a company successful also need to change to adapt to these new circumstances. This often involves changing the way the organization thinks and behaves—its culture.

When leaders want to change the culture, they may focus on changing some of the artifacts (things you can see or feel) or espoused values (how people explain the values of the organization and the reason behind why they do things the way they do). For example, if the leader wants the company to become more innovative, they might change the way they talk, emphasizing creativity and bringing forth new ideas. Or they might change their mission statement to reflect their new focus on innovation. They might also change the way their offices are configured to encourage people to have the chance encounters that often spark creativity and innovation. Or they might hire people with different backgrounds and skill sets toward this goal. If you were to see these artifacts or hear these espoused values, you might think, "Hey, this culture has really changed!"

But has it? Changing the artifacts and espoused values may make it look as if the culture has changed, but unless the organization addresses the ways people think and behave, going to the level of shared tacit assumptions, it may have only made cosmetic changes without fundamentally changing the culture. Because shared tacit assumptions are taken for granted and deeply engrained in how the organization thinks and works, they can be challenging to even understand, let alone alter. And this is why organizational culture can be difficult to change. For example, if there are deeply held beliefs that risk is scary or that mistakes should be punished or that certain conversations shouldn't occur, then creating a culture of innovation may be complicated, and the espoused values of innovation won't match the actual behaviors. It's in cases like this that we see the espoused values, what the organization says about what it values, not matching the enacted values, the actual behaviors, which reflect what the firm *actually* values, and its shared tacit assumptions. In situations like this, employees pay more attention to what people do and the actions and behaviors that are rewarded (or punished) than to what the organization and its leaders say about the organization's values. This is why culture change can be very difficult—it's hard to change the way people in an organization think and behave.

Although organizational culture is notoriously difficult to change, there are examples of successful culture change. One such example comes from Microsoft. Founded in 1975 by Bill Gates and Paul Allen, it's Bill Gates we think of when we think about the early years of Microsoft, and he certainly had a large impact on the company's culture. Cerebral, forward-thinking, fiercely competitive, driven, and combative, he was also known for his intense, all-consuming work ethic. Within the company, Gates was both revered and feared. Michael Gartenberg, an analyst at Gartner Group, summed up the culture this way: "The Microsoft corporate culture can be broken down into four key parts: a tremendous work ethic; Bill Gates is always right; an us-versus-them mentality; and Bill Gates is always right."[7]

On January 13, 2000, Gates stepped down as CEO, and Steve Ballmer, an early employee of Microsoft, took over. A 2012 article described the culture at Microsoft under Ballmer:

> What began as a lean competition machine led by young visionaries of unparalleled talent had mutated into something bloated and bureaucracy-laden, with an internal culture that unintentionally rewards managers who strangle innovative ideas that might threaten the established order of things . . . life behind the thick corporate walls had become staid and brutish. Fiefdoms had taken root, and a mastery of internal politics emerged as key to career success. . . . Staffers were rewarded not just for doing well but for making sure that their colleagues failed. As a result, the company was consumed by an endless series of internal knife fights. Potential market-busting businesses—such as e-book and smartphone technology—were killed, derailed, or delayed amid bickering and power plays.[8]

Ballmer attempted to change the culture, announcing a reorganization to realign the company so it could innovate with greater speed, efficiency, and capability in the rapidly changing technology market and remake Microsoft into an organization that was "Nimble, Communicative, Collaborative, Decisive, and Motivated."[9] However, Ballmer was ultimately unsuccessful in altering the culture or changing the shared tacit assumptions, and he resigned on August 23, 2013.

Satya Nadella took over as CEO of Microsoft in February 2014. Known to be warm, empathetic, curious, humble, and a skilled communicator, Nadella was viewed as the virtual opposite of Gates and Ballmer. He realized that it would be a big job to change the culture from one with warring factions that not only made Microsoft a difficult place to work but also crippled innovation.[10]

What did he do? Many things. And here are some of the most impactful ones: On his first day as CEO, Nadella sent out a letter to all Microsoft employees, beginning by saying, "Today is a very humbling day for me," and remarking on how it reminded him of his first day at Microsoft, twenty-two years earlier. The letter went on to tell a little about himself and how he was at Microsoft for the same reason others were: "to change the world through technology that empowers people to do amazing things." He also mentioned that it was a critical time for Microsoft and how the organization needed to prioritize innovation and drive culture change by focusing on finding meaning in the work they do, which was focused on improving other people's lives.[11] He aimed to connect people with the purpose of the organization to tap into their intrinsic motivation.

Nadella also embarked on a "listening tour," meeting with and listening to many of the thirty-nine thousand Microsoft employees throughout the world, as well as key Microsoft partners, before making any changes to the company's strategy. He opened lines of communication and got Microsoft working with some of its fiercest longtime rivals, including Oracle and Apple, a move that shocked many veteran Microsoft employees. He asked his leadership team to read Marshall Rosenberg's *Nonviolent Communication: A Language of Life* and focused them on treating people with respect. He also created a seventeen-person team of leaders to define what a new culture would mean for Microsoft, and he later replaced people on the leadership team who couldn't adapt to the new culture, a move that was both strategic in changing the culture and symbolic to the entire organization.

And, of course, he did many other things, including sending a multitude of communications, changing processes, and modeling the change. The culture at Microsoft began to change, and as it changed, the organization saw higher employee engagement, lower turnover, higher levels of innovation, and a resulting strong financial performance. Nadella did something very hard—he changed the culture and unleashed the talent to focus on innovation and solving customer problems rather than competing internally. Wall Street noticed too, sending Microsoft's stock price soaring.

The culture that Nadella inherited had been like Gates—hard-charging, fiercely competitive, argumentative, blunt, and valuing winning above all else. Gates's leadership style emerged from his life experiences just as Nadella's leadership style emerged from his. And both men created cultures that reflected these experiences and their values. As CEO, Nadella was Microsoft's chief culture officer and a culture maker who had the power to enact four levers for evolving a culture: (1) articulating the intention for culture change, as well as the outcomes of that change; (2) selecting and developing leaders who align with the new ways of working; (3) using organizational conversations about culture to shift the shared norms and beliefs; and (4) reinforcing the change through redesigning the structures and systems.[12] As Nadella and others who have successfully changed an organizational culture might tell you, embarking on a culture-change initiative is not for the faint of heart.

Assessing an Organization's Culture to Determine Fit

Because organizational culture is relatively stable and slow to change, particularly in older and larger organizations, it's important to understand the culture of an organization in which you work or are considering joining to discern whether it's a place where you are likely to thrive. Here are four categories to help you begin to understand a culture you are already a part of or might consider joining:

What Artifacts Do You Observe?

What do you observe? This includes office decor, how clean or cluttered offices and desks appear, whether the environment is quiet or loud, whether there are private offices or an open floor plan, and what appear to be the "trappings" of success (e.g., executive parking spaces, luxury cars in the parking lot, executive dining room, office size or location). It includes the general vibe as well. The environment may feel energetic, cerebral, social, efficient, genial, or tense. Are the people in positions of power similar (e.g., gender, race, educational background, style) to one another or different? Do people dress formally or informally, or do some groups, or people at different levels in the hierarchy, dress more formally than others? Think about what each of these observations may mean and how you react to an environment that exhibits these qualities. What types of people succeed here? What you observe speaks to what the organization values, whether everyone is expected to be egalitarian or hierarchical, how they define success, how they reward people, et cetera. Nap pods, showers, fully stocked kitchens, game tables, dry-cleaning services, menstrual products in the bathroom, and a company cafeteria may indicate an organization that cares about their employees' comfort and well-being or a company that expects employees to work long hours and provides these amenities to make it easier for people to do so without leaving the office. If this is an organization you're considering joining, pay attention to what you observe, particularly what surprises you, for these surprises may be worth further investigation.

How Do People Behave Toward Others?

What can you see regarding how people interact with one another? This includes how people treat visitors and new employees, whether they tend to their comfort (e.g., offering coffee or water, asking to take their coat) or not. Are people formal or informal with one another? Are some people more deferential? Are people very animated when talking to others or more subdued? Do people yell, swear, or behave aggressively or condescendingly toward others? In meetings, do one or two people dominate discussions, or does everyone weigh in with ideas and comments? Do you hear laughter? What might these behaviors say about the culture and what types of people are attracted to the organization, and what types of people thrive there?

How Do People Describe the Culture?

How do you, the people you work with, or those you are interviewing with interpret the artifacts (e.g., open floor plan, clean desks, free snacks, shower), as well as the words that people would use to describe the culture and what succeeds in that culture (and doesn't)? For example, sometimes having a shower in the office means that the organization values people who take good care of themselves and work out, so they provide showers to make it easier. Other organizations provide showers because people work long hours or take overnight flights, and the company would rather have them come directly into the office to freshen up rather than going home. Ditto with fully stocked kitchens and places to sleep during the day (e.g., nap rooms).

Dig deeper into some of the words used to describe the culture. For example, if you and others describe the organization as a family, what is meant by this? Describing a culture as like a family might mean many things, such as that it's hierarchical, that decision-making is done at the top and everyone is expected to comply, that "siblings" fight and the "parents" (management) mediate disputes, that the organization is paternalistic, or any other such family dynamic. Describing an organization as "work hard, play hard" can also have many potential interpretations. For example, it might mean that the expectation is that people work hard and then release tension through a hard-partying culture or that the "play-hard" part is done as a group or on your own. It could also mean that the organization really means "work hard" and that the "play-hard" part is just assumed to be up to you. What is the meaning behind the words used to describe organizational culture and values?

Who Are the Organization's Heroes?

A telling aspect of culture is who the organization celebrates and the stories people in the company tell about them. These people are celebrated, sometimes even revered, because they embody the deep values, the shared tacit assumptions, of the organization. Heroes may be talked about because they "saved" the company or a client or project, and therefore embody the values of the organization. In Carla's example, her client's organization celebrated people who could "put out fires." Other organizations have different types of heroes. For example, MIT celebrates independent thinkers and those who had the persistence and courage of their convictions to change the world or extend the boundaries of current thinking. And at Microsoft, heroes went from aggressive work-all-the-time political warriors who jockeyed to show how smart they were to more respectful, collaborative innovators who focus on both performance and learning. Who are the heroes in your organization or in the organization you're considering joining? What do the heroes reflect about the organization's culture?

If you are currently leading an organization, you can use the above four categories to gain insight into your organizational culture. And if you are already part of an organization, you can use these categories to understand and evaluate your company's culture for personal fit.

Some Questions to Ask to Determine Fit

If you are considering joining an organization, here are some questions you can select from to ask your interviewer to help better understand the organization's culture:

- What words would you use to describe the culture?
- What metaphors might you use to describe the culture?
- When you joined the organization, what surprised you?

- What stories about people or events does everyone here know and tell to others?
- Can you tell me about your organizational "heroes," or who is celebrated, rewarded, and promoted? What is it that they do, or did, that makes them a hero in the organization?
- What's your favorite workplace tradition?
- Can you tell me about the founder and how their values and ways of working may still be evident in the culture today?
- What do you like best about the culture?
- What about the culture might you like to change?
- What is it about me that makes you think I'd be a good fit here?

There are no good or bad answers to the above questions. However, some answers may resonate with you, and others may repel you—and this is a good thing. Having done the self-understanding work in Chapter 3, you can use the answers you hear to better understand whether the organization might be a good fit for you.

Should I Stay or Should I Go?

Just as one of the most common questions I get from students and participants is about whether they should leave their current boss, another popular question is about whether they should leave a certain organizational culture. Again, the answer is "It depends," and the questions you might ask yourself are similar to those about leaving a manager:

- Which elements of the culture (e.g., aspects of the artifacts, espoused values, and shared tacit assumptions) appeal to me?
- How well do my values align with the organization's enacted values?
- What does it take to succeed in this organization? Is this something that aligns with my values and definition of success?
- Are there people within the organization I admire and would like to become more like?
- Is working in this organization negatively affecting my mental health?
- What have I learned about myself from this organization and its culture that might help me find a better fit next time?

If you find yourself in a culture that isn't a good fit for you, it may be time to actively seek a new job in an organization whose culture is a better fit for you.

Making the Best of a Bad Situation

Even if we want to leave an organization, there may be times when leaving may not be a viable short-term solution. In these situations, it can be helpful to focus on what you can learn while you remain there, which may include taking on new projects or challenges, networking widely within the company, or practicing dealing with demanding people or trying situations. However, staying in a culture that is not a good fit comes with an emotional and sometimes physical toll as we must rally each day just to get through it.

In addition, an organization's culture may change you. We humans adapt to our circumstances, and when we adapt to culture, it can change the way we work, the way we think, the way we behave, and the way we lead. If you join a mean-spirited organization, to do well there you may need to develop sharp elbows. If you join an organization that rewards talent and outcomes more than learning, be prepared for learning how to pretend you know things that you don't know, hiding mistakes for fear of punishment, and navigating a competitive, often political culture. If you join a company that has a culture of learning and support, you will likely improve your skills, develop professionally, and be encouraged to help others grow.

Different organizations have different cultures, and some of these cultures are more suited to our values and ambitions than others. As culture takers, which most people working for various organizations are, we are socialized into the culture, and understanding how a company approaches problems and what behaviors and people are rewarded or punished helps us choose an organization wisely. Because company culture determines what ideas are heard, whose ideas are considered, how rewards are distributed, and, ultimately, who succeeds, most cultures have aspects that are desirable and aspects that are less desirable. The question is whether you think you can survive and thrive in that environment. Just as two different plants may need different amounts of sunshine or water or different types of soil or temperature to thrive, different people will thrive in different cultures. Understanding an organization's culture can help us plant ourselves where we will grow.

8

Unpacking the Challenges of Leadership

Shailesh Shukla was about a year into his tenure as vice president of strategy and business development at a midsize Silicon Valley start-up and had a tough decision to make: What would he say to the board? Having spent many years in strategy consulting, he was used to doing analysis and recommendations for what companies should do. But now he was doing this analysis for his own firm, and the recommendation his analysis pointed to was giving him pause. According to Shailesh, "Thirty percent of the company's R&D was in one product portfolio, the company's original business, and my analysis told me that the market for this category was going to shrink and products like ours would eventually be incorporated into other products." In other words, this product was not going to grow, and the market for it would ultimately go away. "People told me to just lay out the facts but not give my recommendation. But the more I looked at the data, the more I couldn't do that." The company founders and engineers believed deeply in the product and its future potential, but that's not what Shailesh was seeing: "Several people told me I shouldn't stand up and say we should kill the product and that doing so might cost me my job." But that's what he did. "I presented all the data, then told the board that I thought the work in this area should be stopped, that we should sell that part of the business, and redirect the R&D spend and the engineering time to work on other promising products." The founders, who were also in the meeting, were surprised that Shailesh went ahead with his recommendation and responded by telling him that he was new to the company, new to the business, and didn't really understand because he'd never built a business before. "Walking out of the meeting," Shailesh told me, "I wasn't sure I would have a job the next day." However, unbeknownst to Shailesh, one of the board members had been coming to a similar conclusion but hadn't yet publicly said so: "We ended up selling that unit, and I kept my job for many more years—and many other tough decisions there. That experience was a big lesson for me about standing up for what I think is right and having the courage of my convictions."

Having the courage of our convictions, sometimes going against conventional wisdom or even the advice of well-meaning people, and making decisions that not everyone agrees with—these situations encapsulate some of the challenges inherent in leadership. There is rarely a single right answer to almost any question in leadership. The most truthful answer to most questions in leadership is "It depends." This is because good answers, and good solutions, depend on the context of the situation—and the context is continually changing. Markets shift, new technologies emerge, and consumer habits change. When we're talking about situations or decisions involving people, which we are when we talk about leadership, "It depends" is particularly true.

Instead of asking "What's the right answer?" or "What should I do?" we're often better served by asking "What are my options, and what are the consequences of these options?" We can then analyze these options, considering the unique context of the situation, the goals and priorities in the organization, the people involved, and our own values to unpack the challenge and find a solution we're comfortable with.

The Responsibility of a Leader

Leadership involves harnessing the collective knowledge and energy of people on our teams and in our organizations to solve big, important problems. It's a huge job that involves a dizzying number of decisions about issues large and small. Our job as a leader is to improve outcomes, which is usually a combination of financial performance, stakeholder satisfaction, and creating the conditions for the organization to thrive in the future. And there are trade-offs in doing this. Many, many trade-offs. The important part of this is that we take into consideration not just the goal we're pursuing but also what trade-offs we are making in the decision process. Often, how we get to an outcome can be as important as reaching that outcome, and this is why understanding our values is important in decision-making. A spreadsheet may lead us toward a certain decision, but what we ultimately decide will reveal our values.

No decision that we make as leaders will make everyone happy. This is something for us all to become more comfortable with, but it's not always easy. Many years ago, when I was leading the MBA program at MIT, we conducted research into our admissions processes and found that we had an opportunity to revolutionize the way we marketed the program and selected students. Unfortunately, the research results came in just as we were launching a new cycle, which meant that we could either wait until the next admissions cycle, a year later, to implement the findings or make significant changes to our process right away and then make smaller adjustments later as we learned more about what was working and what wasn't working. I made the unpopular decision to move forward with implementing the changes in the current year, which meant modifying some of our internal processes, changing the way we interviewed candidates, updating how we used data in our decisions, and altering how we ran admissions-decision meetings. It was no small project, and several of the people on the team were upset that we didn't wait. They wanted to study the situation more and come up with the "right" protocols for the next year. However, I believed the best way to learn quickly was to implement and adjust as we went. Because it was ultimately my decision, this is the way we proceeded, and I was persona non grata with several members of the admissions team until the results started coming in, showing that our yields on the students we most wanted to come to MIT had increased significantly. We made some further adjustments to our processes for the next year, based on what we'd learned from the prior year, and in the new year our pool of high-quality applicants increased, as did our yields. Difficult decisions, particularly ones that involve trade-offs and result in some people being unhappy, are also part of leadership.

Determining which problems are worthy of our attention and the mindshare of our employees is a hallmark of leadership effectiveness, and leading at higher levels in the organization involves a change in our perspective. We go from problem-solving to problem-finding, and then to prioritizing the most important problems to solve. As we rise through levels in the organization, we begin to see the bigger picture and the longer-term implications for the decisions we make today and the options, or prisons, that result from these decisions. We go from taking a functional view to an enterprise view. Having a sense of what we are trying to accomplish and what we are trading off in pursuing these goals helps us make the *appropriate* trade-offs and be able to communicate our decisions to those who are affected.

It Depends

During the debrief for an exercise I run in workshops, where many of the teams fail to meet their objective, I play a video that discusses why this is often true. In the video, the speaker says this is because "business students are taught to find the single right answer." And it's not just business students. In school, most of the problems we were asked to solve have a "right" answer, which often feels comforting. As humans, we crave certainty. However, there is rarely a single right answer, particularly when we are talking about working with people. Yet many media reports that highlight research make it appear that there is more certainty in the findings than the investigators themselves would conclude. As researchers tell us, "Rarely, if ever, in research will all in one group exhibit the same behavior or opinion. There really are no findings that are true 100 percent of the time; there are always variations when it comes to actual human beings. . . . Research findings should be discussed . . . with words like 'tend to' or 'more likely' and 'less likely' rather than 'are' or 'are not.'"[1] For example, if a report comes out that says "consumption of 3 to 5 standard cups of coffee daily has been consistently associated with a reduced risk of several chronic diseases,"[2] this does not mean that everyone who drinks three to five cups of coffee each day will not develop one of these chronic illnesses. It means that they are *more likely* to not develop these diseases, not that they *won't* develop these diseases. In fact, many of them will develop those diseases, but at a lower rate than those who do not drink coffee.

Much of the research, particularly psychology or sociology research, or any research with human subjects, can help you see patterns but can't help you predict results with any given person or group. Just because 90 percent of people in the research study responded similarly, we can't say that the findings will hold for the people in front of us. We can't predict anyone else's behavior with complete accuracy, and although research can help us understand large patterns of behavior, predicting any individual's actions or behavior is generally not possible.[3] Research gives us probabilities, not certainties. So what's the right answer? It depends.

Effective leadership doesn't have easy answers. It turns out that two situations we face are never truly the same, so the answer is unlikely to always be the same. The context changes—perhaps it's a different person in a situation we've seen before or the same person in a different situation. Or perhaps it's a similar situation in a different company, or industry, or at a different time in the organization's life. When the context changes, as it constantly does, our decisions may very well change. As Heraclitus said, "No man ever steps in the same river twice, for it's not the same river and he's not the same man."

Challenges in Leadership

In leading people and organizations, there are a myriad of decisions to make. For our purposes, we'll look at three types of challenging decisions we face as leaders: problems, dilemmas, and paradoxes. All these challenges require thought and skill to address, but how we approach them may be different.

Problems

Problems are situations that must be somehow resolved, and although there may be multiple viable solutions, there is often not a single right answer. However, some answers may be better than others. For example, there are multiple answers to questions like these: How can we cut costs? How can we reduce employee turnover? How can we increase productivity? How should we market this new product? Should we hire this candidate or search more broadly for someone with more experience? These decisions involve trade-offs and may involve winners and losers. However, with a problem, once you choose an option to pursue, that problem has been resolved, and you can move on.

All decisions have consequences, and it's helpful to consider what they will be up front. This way you can prepare for them and avoid, or mitigate, some of the downsides. You may still need to make a difficult decision that will negatively affect some people, but carefully considering the options, the possible consequences, and how we may ultimately approach and announce the decision can help us make a better, more informed decision.

When looking at the various options, which one, or which combination, solves the problem most effectively? One straightforward way to analyze alternatives is encapsulated in the "Choosing Among Alternatives" framework (Figure 8). You can download the template for your own use at www.margaretandrews.com/mylobookresources.

A Framework for Evaluating Alternatives

Option A	Option B	Option C
Pro/Benefits	Pro/Benefits	Pro/Benefits
Con/Drawbacks	Con/Drawbacks	Con/Drawbacks
How We Might Mitigate Cons	How We Might Mitigate Cons	How We Might Mitigate Cons

Figure 8. Choosing Among Alternatives

To analyze a problem, you may want to start with Option A and list all the benefits you can think of for this option. Then, assuming you choose Option A, what are the potential drawbacks, the potential cons, of choosing this alternative? And then, if you were to choose Option A and run into some of these drawbacks, are there ways to mitigate these drawbacks? Then do the same for all other options under consideration. Often we have a preferred option in mind and have a harder time coming up with the potential drawbacks of that option or have trouble finding the possible benefits of the other alternatives. So in filling out a template like this, it's helpful to talk with others, particularly those who have a different preference or are from another part of the organization, to help you consider the alternatives more carefully. This also helps with unintended consequences or "surprises" in choosing and implementing any of the options. Sometimes we may choose an option where we are best equipped to manage the cons.

For more challenging problems, we may need to think more holistically about the issue, including a longer list of potential options and their trade-offs and possible consequences, a better understanding of who will be affected by the decision, what it will take to implement the decision effectively, and how best to communicate the resolution of the issue. Mary Rowe, who teaches at MIT and was MIT's ombuds for many years, has a saying that is helpful in these situations: "Whose interests are at stake, and what are those interests?" I've built upon Rowe's query to create a framework of questions that can be helpful in thinking through difficult decisions:

1. What is my goal in this situation?
2. What am I optimizing for in this decision? And by optimizing for this, what am I therefore trading off, or deprioritizing?
3. What are my options for how to proceed?
4. For each of these options:
    - To what extent does this option address the goal I'm trying to achieve?
    - Who will be affected by choosing this option, both directly and indirectly?

- How might people *perceive* this option, in terms of how it affects them and others? Based on this perception, how might they *feel* about it? What might they *think* about this alternative and its impact?
- What are the potential long-term implications of choosing this option, both positive and negative (e.g., enables or cuts off various future options)?
- Who would need to be involved in the planning and implementation of this option to increase the likelihood of success?

5. Which option, or combination of options, gets us closest to our goal and has manageable trade-offs or downsides?
6. Who needs to know about this decision, and when do they need to know about it?
7. How might I communicate the decision to each affected person or group to increase understanding and support?

Knowing our values and priorities can help us make the difficult trade-offs, as Jen Owings, an assistant principal and instructional-support systems administrator for the Department of Education in New York City, found out. According to Jen, "I had to come to terms that not everyone is going to be happy with my decisions." When putting together the master schedule for the school, "you're never making everyone happy because you've got a lot of people that are impacted by that schedule. I talk to a lot of people, balance the trade-offs, and try to make the best decision I can and then be explicit in sharing the 'why' behind my decision." Balancing the needs of students, teachers, school administrators, and parents is never an easy task:

> I went into education because I care about the kids, and that's a core value I use in making decisions. In my field, if I make decisions in the best interest of kids and my school as a whole, I can't go far wrong. We're in the business of supporting kids, not making adults comfortable. On several occasions my decisions did not align with my superiors' interests, and even when I've been questioned or mildly reprimanded, I've *never* experienced a negative consequence for putting the kids first when making a decision. I can always explain the "why" behind the decision. The older I get, the more I realize the importance of living and leading with integrity. Not only does my reputation depend upon it, but I'm the one who has to live with myself when making these difficult decisions.

Dilemmas

Dilemmas are vexing problems involving a difficult, undesirable, or unpleasant choice between two unsatisfactory alternatives with known and important trade-offs. Some common dilemmas involve unpleasant trade-offs between people and profits or between the rights of different people or groups. For example, should you retain a brilliant scientist who bullies and harasses others? Promote a high-producing salesperson who plays fast and loose with the truth in selling to clients? Hire the client's son even though he is significantly less qualified than other candidates? Close a local plant, negatively affecting those employees and the local economy, and offshore production to save the company millions of dollars? Announce a large layoff or ask everyone in the company to take a pay cut? Although some of these questions and the resulting decisions may sound clear-cut, with a "right" answer, there are often very compelling arguments on both sides. For example, in the opening story in the Introduction to this book, where James raised his hand, we were discussing a case about a brilliant surgeon with terrible interpersonal skills and whether we should keep him or fire him. There were impassioned and reasonable arguments on both sides of the discussion. What sounds like an easy, clear-cut decision is often more nuanced, with difficult trade-offs.

Some of the biggest dilemmas, ones that create the most discussion in class, involve knowing if and when to let an employee go. Should we try to help them improve or cut our losses? When is too soon to decide? "It's hard to know when it's time to call it quits," Shaun Carver, the executive director of International House at UC Berkeley, told me. Shaun was talking about the investment it takes to develop others: "I can be impatient when people are underperforming, and it's difficult to know whether, when this happens, I'm realizing that they may not be interested in improving, unable to improve, or whether it's just me being impatient. I can definitely point to times I've tried coaching someone well beyond the point where I could see it wasn't working, and I'm sure I've given up on some people too quickly."

Another keep-or-cut dilemma can arise when an employee makes an error in judgment that gives us pause about their integrity. Are there some transgressions that should be overlooked, and, if so, which ones and by whom? Many years ago, John Reed, former head of Citibank, told a story about calling one of his lieutenants, a senior executive, into his office and firing him on the spot. Incredulous, the man asked why, and Reed told him: "I just reviewed your expense report and noticed that you had an expense for a $12 cab ride on the day we had a meeting with a client in midtown." The man seemed surprised and, a bit warily, nodded his head, acknowledging the expense item. "You didn't take a cab back to the office. I was with you at that meeting, and we walked back to the office together. And yet there's a $12 cab ride on your expense report for that day." Puzzled, the man told Reed, "I can't believe you're firing me over a $12 expense!" to which Reed replied that of course he was firing him over a $12 fraudulent expense. "If you would risk your job over a $12 charge, it makes me wonder what you would do if real money was involved. I just can't take that risk, so yes, you're fired."

What might we have done if we were in Reed's shoes? On one hand, the person he was firing was an experienced executive, someone whose analysis and advice Reed relied on to run the business. On the other hand, that employee had committed an act of fraud. A small act of fraud, but an act of fraud. It effectively illustrates a dilemma—it's a difficult decision that has implications for whatever you decide. Reed could have looked the other way, noting that $12 is immaterial in the grand scheme of things. He could then avoid losing a very talented employee with deep experience, but he would also be complicit in the fraud and condoning it by his inaction.

Reed could have reprimanded the man but not fired him. The upside of this would be retaining a talented employee. The downside is that he would have allowed someone to commit fraud. In addition, Reed had lost trust in the man and his judgment. And trust is essential. How large a transgression would be in the "acceptable, reprimand them only" range, and what would cross over into the "unacceptable, fire them" range?

Reed could also fire the employee, as he did. The upside of this decision is that the employee would not commit any further transgressions, and his firing would send a strong signal to the organization about ethics and judgment. On the downside, it took a long time to replace the executive, given his level of expertise, which was difficult for the company. And his firing took a toll on the man himself, as well as his family.

You may have decided differently, and that's the thing about dilemmas: There is no absolute right answer. Different people will come to different conclusions and make different decisions. Being clear on our values, which we explored in Chapter 3, is particularly helpful when facing a dilemma. Although dilemmas are either/or propositions that have a "damned if you do, damned if you don't" feel to them, if we have a firm grasp on our own values, reason through the decision, understanding the values at stake as well as the trade-offs on both sides of the issue, we can stand up for the decision, even if others disagree.

Paradoxes

Most challenges in leadership are not clear-cut. Although many are presented as black-and-white, yes-or-no, either/or decisions, many of them are not. Unlike problems and dilemmas, paradoxes aren't solved or resolved. They're managed. We don't "pick a side" on a paradox but rather try to integrate the best of both sides, or poles, of a paradox and create a dynamic balance, one that will need continued monitoring and adjusting. I often call these "gray" challenges because they defy black-and-white solutions and, rather than focusing on the black-and-white alternatives, our best approach is to jump into the gray space. It's like F. Scott Fitzgerald wrote in his 1945 book, *The Crack-Up*: "The test of a first-rate intelligence is the ability to hold two opposed ideas in mind at the same time, and still retain the ability to function."

"One of the paradoxes I find most interesting is the 'Don't sweat the small stuff versus it's the details that matter most.' It, of course, depends on the situation and from whose perspective you're looking at it. It may be a small detail to me, but it may be a big deal to you," Eric Cornell, a former MYLO student and two-time Tony Award–winning Broadway producer, told me:

> In the entertainment field, there's a lot of big thinking and big picture, and yet it can be the small things that make the difference. We're not just selling theater or even entertainment; we're selling an *experience.* The small stuff often has a human element to it, whether it's sending a thank-you note to people that helped along the way, paying attention to the small details in the set design that only a connoisseur would notice, or how people will use your product or experience your service. A great example of this happened when I visited the costume shop that was working on the costumes for a show I was working on, and they showed me how they were making a medallion for the costumes. It was a military costume, and they wanted to ensure the medals were historically accurate, so they got the real medallions and then re-created them in silicone to accommodate not just the dramaturgical elements but the human ones. That designer understood that actors need costumes that look real, cannot be too heavy or too hot, can be put on and off quickly, and can be washed eight times each week without falling apart. Her team was sweating what many people would think are small things, and they were big things for the production and the actors wearing the costumes. Her attention

to this seemingly small detail was important for us, and I think she was proud of that work too. Attention to the details that matter to others shows our stewardship of care for the people we serve.

Paradoxes are rife in organizational life and in just about every aspect of leading. For example, here are a few of the paradoxes in various aspects of leadership (showing the two sides, or poles, that are often presented):

- **Paradoxes in Leading Organizations**
    - long-term vision—short-term results
    - high quality—low cost
    - control—flexibility
    - efficiency—innovation
    - stability—change

- **Paradoxes in Leading People and Projects**
    - holding people accountable—offering grace
    - results-oriented—people-oriented
    - focus on big picture—attention to details
    - sense of urgency—deliberative
    - open-door policy—doing deep work

In managing paradoxes, what we seek is a dynamic balance, akin to how a tightrope walker makes many small adjustments as they traverse the rope. These small adjustments occur throughout the walk as the walker attempts to stay in balance, moving their arms as well as the muscles in their legs, ankles, and feet to adjust to moment-by-moment conditions, which often cannot be known in advance.

Jumping into the gray involves considering the two ends, the two poles, or the two sides of the paradox and then using creativity and insight to examine ways to turn what looks like an either/or situation into a both/and situation. Leadership itself is a creative endeavor, and Teresa Amabile of Harvard Business School found that individual creativity is a combination of expertise, creative thinking skills, and motivation.[4]

Expertise in the creativity context means intellectual knowledge of any sort—your technical knowledge, functional expertise, or even what you know about history, motorcycle maintenance, cooking, or anything else. Creativity is about making connections so that anything you know is fodder for creative ideas. In looking at paradoxes, our expertise in the business, the market context, and the people involved helps us think about potential ways to manage the paradox.

Creative thinking skills relate to how flexibly and imaginatively you can approach a problem. What are all the ways you can think of to address the challenge? What might work? What would definitely not work? It can be helpful to think of these definitely-wouldn't-work ideas as well because sometimes thinking about a "bad" or unworkable idea can lead us to a good, workable idea. You can ask yourself how others might address the situation, people such as your Best Boss, Mother Teresa, Walt

Disney, Tina Fey, Batman, Richard Branson, Maya Angelou, or any other person, real or imagined, to give you more ideas.

Motivation refers to the drive you bring to solving the problem, and it comes in two flavors: extrinsic and intrinsic. Extrinsic motivation comes from outside yourself, and it's easy to think of it as either a carrot or a stick. For example, a carrot would be getting a bonus if you come up with a creative idea, and a stick might be getting a pay cut if you don't. Intrinsic motivation, on the other hand, comes from within. People who are intrinsically motivated work on problems not for accolades or financial rewards but because they are personally interested in finding a solution to the problem. The challenge itself is motivating. Intrinsic motivation turns out to be more important for creativity than extrinsic motivation. People who just want to figure it out are more likely to figure it out than people who are motivated by either carrots or sticks.

For example, when there was an explosion in space and it was unclear if Mission Control would be able to get the astronauts from *Apollo 13* home, it was the engineers and scientists who worked nearly nonstop for many days to bring them down safely. It wasn't a bonus or bragging rights that had these people working relentlessly; it was their intrinsic motivation. These were scientists and engineers who like to solve big, important problems, and it was their friends who were in danger, so they wanted to help them return home. Extrinsic motivation doesn't necessarily work against creative problem-solving, but it's intrinsic motivation that is most helpful.

When addressing a paradox, we can ask ourselves the following questions:

1. Looking at one of the poles, or sides, what are the benefits of this approach?
2. If we focus solely on this pole, or side, what negatives may come up?
3. Looking at the other pole, what are the benefits of this approach?
4. If we focus solely on this other pole, what negatives may come up?
5. What are *all* the ways we can think of to gain the benefits of both poles (answers to questions 1 and 3)?
6. What are *all* the ways we can think of to minimize the negatives of both poles (answers to questions 2 and 4)?

As leaders, "jumping into the gray" using the above questions can help us harness the knowledge and insights of our teams, wrestle with some of the difficult choices in leadership, and find creative ways to manage the context-specific issues we face.

"Before I became a CEO," Shailesh Shukla, CEO of Aryaka, a six-hundred-person software firm in Silicon Valley, told me, "I made some pretty big decisions in other jobs, but it was different." Shailesh had been the number two person in a start-up and had run large businesses in big companies, and he told me that these were supported decisions, where they had a certain process for coming to a decision, a framework, and there were checks and balances on the process: "So, while those decisions may have been important and critical, they didn't fundamentally change the company. But now, as the CEO, all the easier decisions have been made by other people in the organization, and only the really hard decisions reach my desk. The decisions I make now do change the company, and they can impact individuals in the company, as well as their families, and that's a lot of responsibility. Some of these decisions will not be popular, and some may prove to be wrong, but I still have to make those decisions in a timely manner." Indeed. Making good decisions is among the most powerful and difficult challenges in leadership.

You may not always be right, and some of your decisions will not work out as you had hoped. And sometimes changing your mind is a sign of intelligence. As leaders, we will be tested—and judged—by the decisions we make. Many of these decisions will affect other people, both directly and indirectly. And sometimes, even when doing our best, we'll make a bad decision. This happens. Although we can't guarantee that the outcomes of our decisions will be favorable, if we keep our own values and the values of the organization front and center when making decisions, we are more likely to make decisions that we can stand behind.

PART FOUR

Leading for the Long Term

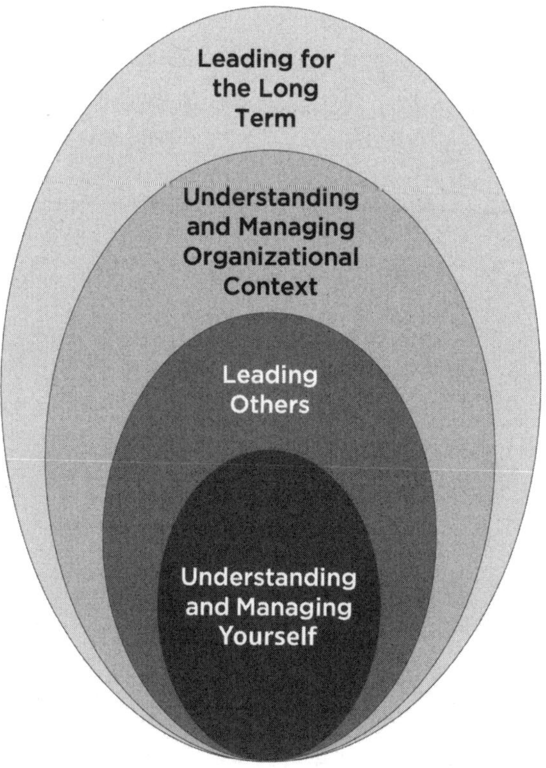

9

Recovering from Setbacks, Getting Unstuck, and Building Resilience

THINGS DIDN'T GO ACCORDING TO plan for Ashwin Damera when, from his home base in India, he started the online travel services company Travelguru: "We were about to be acquired and had signed all the documents and were awaiting the money to be wired into our account. But the wire transfer didn't go through." Unbeknownst to Ashwin and his team at the time was that Lehman Brothers, a 158-year-old financial services company with nearly twenty-five thousand employees worldwide, had just collapsed, commencing the 2008 financial crisis. They soon found out: "The entire start-up world was shaking, the travel industry was collapsing, our deal to sell the company fell apart, and my company entered a very bad phase." At that point, the company had only enough money to stay solvent for two months, which meant he had to lay people off and take some bridge funding. Later that year there were attacks on the Taj and Oberoi hotels in Mumbai, and the travel business took a further hit. And the bad news continued: "Then one of our largest investors wanted to exit, which upset me because I thought we should build the company for the long term and stay with it through the rough patch, and it was only at this time that I found out that this investor and I were not aligned on our values."

Soon thereafter, Ashwin was forced to sell to another company at a lower valuation:

> That was a really tough time for me because at no point in my professional career had I taken a beating like that, and it gave me a lot to reflect on. That moment when life beats you up the hardest is sometimes the time when you get the most clarity about who you are and what matters to you. I began to realize that I had started that company just to make money and had no special attachment to the travel industry. I did, however, have a strong interest in the health care and education industries, two sectors that have the power to improve human life. With a start-up, there's no guarantee of success, and with so many factors outside of your control, it's somewhat like a roll of the dice on whether or not you'll succeed. I wanted to create a company that, whether it was financially successful or not, I would know that I had done something worthwhile with my life.

Ashwin decided to focus on the education space and is now founder and CEO of two of the most successful ed-tech start-ups, Emeritus and Eruditus. As he told me, "I hadn't wanted to sell the first company, but having to sell it was the best thing to happen because then I stumbled upon something that was far more successful monetarily and has been a much better fit for me as a human."

Sometimes, things don't go according to plan, and this can knock us off-balance. Someone lets us down, embarrasses us, denies us a well-deserved promotion, says one thing and does another, betrays our confidence, or behaves in a way that confuses, frustrates, or hurts us. Or we make a mistake that inconveniences (or injures) others, let someone down, have an angry outburst, don't stand up for what we believe, or say or do something we later regret. Welcome to being a human being. If you are putting yourself out there, as we do in leadership, it's likely that at some point you'll have a setback like the ones mentioned above or even a public failure like going out of business, being fired, or finding yourself publicly humiliated. These things *hurt*.

Recovering from Setbacks

Setbacks are a part of life and leadership, and although these reversals may be inevitable, recovery is not. Often, it's not the setback itself that determines our future but rather how we manage through it, the steps we take once we've had that setback.

My family used to go to Maine each summer for a week of swimming, kayaking, hiking, reading, and relaxing together. The highlight of the week was rafting on the Kennebec River. During the safety briefing the guides discussed the terrain, what to expect, and not only how to stay safe in the raft but what to do if you fell out of the raft and found yourself heading down a Class IV rapid all by yourself. They called it "aggressive self-rescue." As they told us, "No one cares more about your safety than you do, and you should act accordingly." This concept applies well beyond whitewater rafting. In fact, it applies to all the whitewater in our lives. Any setback can send us down our own Class IV emotional rapid. In the grip of a setback, either personal or professional, there are some aggressive self-rescue steps we can take to minimize the power, extent, and duration of the setback:

- **Accept reality.** What just happened? Who is affected? It may be tempting to blame others or circumstances for what just happened, but what was your role in the situation? What is now different from before? What remains the same? Be clear about the events and current outcomes. It's difficult to recover from a setback if we are either in denial about the situation or "catastrophize" and give it more significance than it deserves.

- **Assess which factors are within your control at this point and which are not—and then focus on what you *can* control.** You may not be able to control many factors in the current situation, but you can control how you respond. It's tempting to focus on the aspects that are outside our control, ruminating on what just happened or what we should have said or done. However, this often serves to make matters worse as our anxiety takes over. You may find it helpful to make a list of all the factors that are currently outside your control and those that are within your control. Writing it down helps to get the noise out of your head, calm your anxiety, and help reengage your logical brain. Now you can carefully consider what aspects of the situation might be under your control and then focus only on those aspects. What might you do that could have a positive impact on the situation right now?
- **Put your mask on first.** Failure isn't fatal, so take care of yourself as you work through the situation. This means eating well, sleeping as well as possible under the circumstances, and exercising to bolster both physical and mental health. If you are grappling with a setback the organization is facing, such as losing a major client, not getting the next round of funding, regulation changes, or a major PR disaster, remember the old saying that "you can't pour

from an empty vessel." You can't help others if you are in crisis yourself. To the extent possible, go back to routines or rituals you may have (e.g., going for a run in the morning, brushing your teeth, reading before bed) to reach for some level of normalcy or stability. One thing that is fully under your control is how you take care of yourself. Start by putting your phone down and getting off social media. Sometimes the best thing you can do is go for a walk or take a shower to clear your head, or journal about the emotions that are emerging. This gets those difficult emotions out of your body and onto paper, where you can more aptly deal with them.

- **Consider alternative interpretations.** Resist the impulse to view yourself as a victim or villain, and search for any previously unforeseen positives or possibilities. What might this situation or your new circumstances now enable? Sometimes a setback opens new opportunities, as it did for Ashwin. You can also ask yourself if this situation might be something you will laugh about a few years in the future. Perhaps the situation is a fork in the road rather than the end of the road. Sometimes, taking the long view of the situation can stop us from catastrophizing and may help us see some unseen bright sides, ways forward, or paths toward a new beginning. Sometimes a setback can be both a loss and a potential gain, and without seeing the situation clearly, we may focus only on the loss and wallow in that loss. Consider, as Dev Patel's character, Sonny Kapoor, said in the movie *The Best Exotic Marigold Hotel*, "Everything will be all right in the end. So if it's not all right, then it is not yet the end."

- **Reflect.** A setback or any other type of disappointment is not a failure if you learn something from it. Sand in the oyster creates a pearl—what learnings, or pearls of wisdom, can you take away from this situation? How will you use this newfound knowledge? How might it change your behaviors or actions in the future? In what ways might you or others benefit from these learnings?
- **Tap into your values and what motivates you.** Having a good sense of our values helps enormously with rebounding from setbacks, as does knowing what we like to do. Steve Jobs, in his 2005 commencement address at Stanford University, discussed how devastated he felt after being fired from Apple, the company he started: "What had been the focus of my entire adult life was gone, and it was devastating. I really didn't know what to do for a few months." Feeling that he was not only embarrassed by such a public shaming but also as if he'd let others in the industry down, he considered leaving the industry—until he had a realization that he still

loved the work he did. And this changed the trajectory of his life: "I didn't see it then, but it turned out that getting fired from Apple was the best thing that could have ever happened to me. The heaviness of being successful was replaced by the lightness of being a beginner again, less sure about everything. It freed me to enter one of the most creative periods of my life." During the next several years he started another computer company, invested in a fledgling company called Pixar, and met the woman he would later marry. When Apple bought his computer company, Jobs returned to Apple, and the company went on to launch the iPhone, iPad, and Apple watch. Jobs not only bounced back from a humiliating experience; he also took the lessons and bounced forward into a better position. In reflecting on his experience, Jobs remarked that "it was awful-tasting medicine, but I guess the patient needed it."[1] Although Jobs's story is remarkable, it doesn't need to be. What, at your core, do you care about? What's important to you? What do you enjoy doing? What do you want to accomplish in your life? How might you use this opportunity to move closer to your values?

- **Become a bricoleur.** A bricoleur is someone who engages in bricolage, a term first used by French social anthropologist Claude Lévi-Strauss to mean the skill to create or construct something by using a diverse range of available things. It's about using whatever is handy and doing what you can with what you have. Consider what future options the setback enables. Imagine a different future. What might you do with the situation and the resources you now have? Think creatively to imagine a better future—and then go after this future and begin to create it. Start slowly and see what works.

- **Become the hero in your journey.** In the hero's journey, first popularized by Joseph Campbell, the hero accepts the Call to Adventure and leaves the Ordinary World to enter the Special World, one where they need to learn the rules of this new, unfamiliar world. After a series of trials and tests, the hero encounters the Supreme Ordeal, a very difficult challenge, often their greatest fear that they must face before they can achieve their goal. The hero is not sure they will prevail or even survive the ordeal, but they do, and, long story short, the hero returns home a transformed person. Thinking of our situation this way can give us perspective and cast us as the hero of our journey, in charge of our own destiny. Perhaps this is your Supreme Ordeal to confront and then begin a personal or professional transformation?

Getting Unstuck

Sometimes we feel stuck, lackadaisical, or "meh." It's not that we've had a major setback or disappointment, and it's not exactly burnout, but it may feel like we're stagnating, muddling through, or stuck in place. When we feel this way for an uncomfortably long period of time, which will be different for each one of us, it may be an indication that we need to get closer to what matters to us.

Ben, a senior executive with a New York–based multinational music company, told me this:

> When I came to the Managing Yourself and Leading Others program, I was feeling like I'd lost my creative spark and wanted to get it back. So I asked myself why I got into the music business in the first place, and the answer was that I got into the music business to make records that make people feel something and move. I like to make records that make people dance. However, as I became more senior and moved into executive positions, I moved away from the creative side of the business. And with that move away from the creative side, I'd lost my creative spark, the energy that drives me and makes me good at what I do. I then realized that I needed to carve out time to feed my inspiration and now have a 90-minute block on my calendar each day for what I call "creative flow time." This time is nonnegotiable for me, and I don't do meetings, calls,

> or social media during this time. I just listen to music and think of ideas for improving the music. Then I can send out these creative ideas to my network to catalyze action. I was reluctant to carve out this time on my calendar at first, but have found it's the best, most creative part of my day and that it makes me more creative and productive, as well as happier, the rest of the day. It's put a lot of joy back into my work and reconnected me with the reasons I went into the music business in the first place.

Returning to the Six Questions for Self-Understanding can help us ground ourselves and look back over the people, ideas, and events that helped shape us, as well as our values and definition of success. And we can update our answers. Our values and our aspirations change over our lifetime based on our age and stage in life, personal events, our health, our work life, and other changes in perspective. Often, connecting with ourselves, going inward, and reevaluating our answers to the Six Questions can help us make small adjustments, as Ben did, that help us reconnect with ourselves. These feelings of being stuck may also indicate that it's time for us to do a career pivot or wholesale change. Nadine Kawkabani, a strategy executive in a Boston-based financial services company, told me about her secret to success, which is self-reinvention: "As professionals, we must continually reinvent ourselves. I've reinvented myself multiple times in my career and help people that report to me realize that this is the name of the game, and what will help them to *continue* to succeed."

Building Resilience

Leading people, teams, and units can be exhilarating, challenging, and satisfying. The work can also be relentless, exhausting, and lonely. So let's talk about resilience.

People often think about resilience as "bouncing back" from a disappointment or setback, similar to the way you can stretch a rubber band. Most of the time, when we stretch a rubber band, it returns to its original shape. But if we stretch it too far, it breaks. And if you've ever stretched a rubber band and kept it stretched for too long, it doesn't return to its original shape—it loses its elasticity as well as its usefulness as a rubber band. People can be like this as well, sometimes working too hard for too long, not eating well or getting sufficient sleep or exercise, and accumulating stress until they reach burnout. Fortunately, most people who reach the burnout stage do recover. However, bouncing back may take a long time and can have career and personal implications.

Resilience is often defined as the ability to recover from setbacks, adapt well to change, and keep going in the face of adversity.[2] But resilience isn't just about "bouncing back." According to the American Psychological Association, "Psychologists define resilience as the process of adapting well in the face of adversity, trauma, tragedy, threats, or significant sources of stress—such as family and relationship problems, serious health problems, or workplace and financial stressors. As much as resilience involves 'bouncing back' from these difficult experiences, it can also involve profound personal growth."[3]

Dr. Kati Karikó is an example of resilience. Growing up in Hungary as the daughter of a butcher, she decided at a very young age that she wanted to be a scientist, although she'd never met one. Moving to the United States in her twenties, she stayed on the fringes of academia for decades, never making more than $60,000 per year and moving from lab to lab as her research repeatedly lost funding. Many of the research directors didn't believe her conviction, which went against conventional wisdom in the medical community, that the body's own cells could be used to make their own medicines, including vaccines. A chance encounter with another researcher, Dr. Drew Weissman, changed the course of her career and of history. Their work laid the foundation for the technology used in Pfizer-BioNTech's and Moderna's COVID-19 vaccines, and in 2023 they won the Nobel Prize in Medicine for their research on messenger RNA (mRNA).[4]

Resilience is not just about persisting, persevering, or enduring, although resilience helps you do all these things. It's about what you do to make enduring possible. It involves what to do to take good care of yourself. It's not about being "tough"—it's about being flexible and resourceful. How resilient we are depends on what's in our tool kit, and here are some tools that can help us improve our capacity for resilience:

- **Values, purpose, and meaning.** Understanding our values and goals and making an effort to move toward them can help us maintain perspective and give meaning to our efforts. It can help us focus on what's most important to us and maintain emotional balance. When we have setbacks, understanding our values can help us return to these values, and keeping them front and center may also help us avoid, or recover more quickly from, future setbacks. Rob Duboff, cofounder of Boston-based HawkPartners, is a consummate networker, someone who makes real connections with people that last for decades. Not only this, but he also generously connects people in his network to others whenever that connection would be helpful. I've known Rob for decades, and he's connected me to many people and been generous with advice that has helped me in my career. He's so generous with people that one time I told him I worried about him. I worried that people would take advantage of his kindness and generosity. Rob's response? "Yes," he said, "sometimes I do get taken advantage of, but it doesn't happen very often. I tend to trust people, and I'm usually right in trusting them because most people don't take advantage. And this is the way I want to live my life, working with great people, helping them succeed, and trusting them to do the right thing." For Rob, that's worked out pretty well so far.

- **Self-care.** This includes eating well, getting enough sleep on a regular basis, exercising, and learning to manage stress, which may include taking breaks, tuning out social media, spending time on an enjoyable hobby, or taking time for reflection with yoga, meditation, journaling, or going for a long run. Taking care of ourselves is part of our job because if we can't take care of ourselves, how will we have the physical and emotional resources to lead others?
- **Social.** Maintaining strong personal relationships and having people in our life who are trustworthy helps us maintain balance and perspective, and can be a source of comfort and support when we need them. Beyond our family and friends, we can expand our social circle by joining a community or group, whether it's a civic group, a faith-based community, an academic or personal-enrichment class, or a book club.

Our lives can be shaped by both lucky and unlucky accidents, and when one of these events occurs, it may be hard to know on which side of the ledger it belongs. Connie Askin, CEO of a youth-serving nonprofit organization, got into the nonprofit world through a series of what, at first, seemed to be unlucky events: "A couple of decades ago, I was laid off from an insurance company. I was the highest-performing person in the group, but I was also a highly paid person, and that's why they let me go." It was this experience that made her think of doing something completely different, and she happened to see a posting for a job at AFS, an international study-abroad program, one she had participated in during high school. She decided to call and ask more about the job: "But I called the wrong number. The job I saw was with AFS USA, but I mistakenly called the international office." The person Connie spoke to said that they didn't have a job similar to the one she asked about but that the CFO position was open. "That piqued my interest," Connie told me. Looking online for more information on the organization, she saw a name that looked familiar on the board of directors, someone who lived near her but not someone she knew personally: "I called his office, thinking I'd probably get his assistant, but he ended up picking up the phone, and we spoke for an hour and a half." Connie got the job, and it launched her career in the nonprofit world: "If you're the kind of person who makes the hard choices, things are not always going to go as you had planned. Or maybe you just got caught in the crosswinds of what's happening in the organization. It doesn't really matter what caused the setback; what really matters is how you get back up on your feet, brush yourself off, and decide where to go next."

10

The Long View

CLAIRE, THE VP OF FINANCE for a sports network in Southern California, told me a story, and we came to different conclusions about the moral of the story. As Claire told me, she had a great job in the entertainment industry, but the long workdays and multi-hour commute were arduous: "I had to pack and bring three meals with me each day—breakfast to eat in the car, lunch to eat at my desk, because I was too busy to go out for lunch, and then dinner to also eat at my desk, because I would get home very late, well past dinnertime." Her schedule was not only difficult but also becoming unsustainable. Claire's father had recently passed away, her mother needed help, her husband also had a demanding job and was beginning to travel more frequently, and they had a ten-year-old daughter. "I liked the work I did and the team I'd built over the years, but I just couldn't do this anymore," she told me. Something had to change.

There were two major corporations within a half-hour drive of her house, and because she had in-demand skills and former managers and coworkers who gave her very strong recommendations, she quickly found a position at one of them. Although the new job was minutes from her house and gave her more personal time, it left a lot to be desired on the professional front: "The job was dull, and the office environment was more conservative and quiet than a bank and a library combined." On top of this, her boss was verbally abusive: "The job and the company were a bad fit for me from the start, but because I really needed to be closer to home, I kept at it for several years and was becoming more and more miserable."

A friend of Claire's from a previous job had another friend who had taken on a new CFO position for a start-up and was looking for a controller. He asked Claire's friend if she knew anyone that would be good for the position. "Yep," said her friend, "and she's currently working right across the street from you." Claire took that job, and it became, as she called it, her on-the-job MBA, where she learned about every functional area in the organization: "It was a start-up that needed to get to profitability, so I went into my usual 'little engine that could' mode." Claire got the company through an intensive audit, let go of a few people on her team who were not performing, helped define and execute strategy, and took over her boss's role when he was let go soon after her arrival: "But then the HR director left, and the CEO decided to put that function under me, so now I was the HR director on top of everything else! I knew nothing about that role and realized that my number one priority was filling that job. So I went to my computer and put the position on multiple job boards and then emailed everyone I knew asking if they knew of a good person for this role." Recommendations poured in. "I was really surprised by how many people sent me recommendations," Claire said. The position was filled in less than a month, and she could return to her other roles.

As Claire finished telling me that story, she said, "So I guess the lesson I learned from these experiences is that you cannot predict anything. Sometimes you just have to keep your head down and keep going and it might all work out." I laughed and told her that I heard a very different lesson: How well you work with people is very important in your career. I heard how the people she had worked with, supported, and developed throughout her career were there to support her. She then laughed and told me, "Oh, I didn't really consider that. I think when you work closely with people, you really get to know them, and your colleagues become your friends." I've known Claire for several decades and can attest to her being smart, hardworking, conscientious, and well-intentioned. She is also one of the kindest, most generous people on the planet. So it's no surprise that anyone she'd previously worked with would mention her name as a great person to hire, or if they received an email from her, would not only open the email but also do what they could to help. That's the compound effect of understanding and managing yourself, as well as leading others effectively, over a long period of time. People trust you. They want to help. They will connect you with opportunities. They will lift you up.

There's nothing stopping any of us from understanding and managing ourselves, and leading others well. Nothing, perhaps, but our own fear. Our fear of making a change. Our fear of being different. Our fear of being the best possible version of ourselves.

In 2006 the *Akeelah and the Bee* movie debuted, and I went to watch it on the big screen. It's the story of eleven-year-old Akeelah Anderson, who is a very good speller. Her teacher and school principal want Akeelah to enter the school's first-ever spelling bee. She reluctantly enters the bee and then wins, which qualifies her to participate in the state's regional finals. Along the way, Akeelah meets Dr. Larabee, a distinguished language scholar who believes that Akeelah has the potential to enter the Scripps National Spelling Bee, and he becomes her coach. The movie follows Akeelah's ascent as a speller, the community that comes to support her, and the relationship between Akeelah and Larabee. As you might guess, Akeelah and Larabee learn important lessons from each other.

In one scene, shot in Larabee's office, he asks Akeelah to read from a quotation he has framed on the wall, which begins with "Our deepest fear is not that we are inadequate. Our deepest fear is that we are powerful beyond measure." I remember getting chills as she read those lines. They resonated deeply because I believe those words are true. It's our own potential that most frightens us. We're afraid of just how great we can become.

Later, I kept thinking about these words and wondered if it was a "quote" created for the movie. So I typed those words into a search engine and quickly found that they were not made up for the movie but were from a book, *A Return to Love*, by Marianne Williamson. Searching further, I found the full passage and read through it, smiling at the lines above and continuing on. There was more to the passage, words that resonate with me to this day:

> Our deepest fear is not that we are inadequate. Our deepest fear is that we are powerful beyond measure. It is our light, not our darkness, that most frightens us. We ask ourselves, Who am I to be brilliant, gorgeous, talented, fabulous? Actually, who are you not to be? . . . Your playing small doesn't serve the world. There's nothing enlightening about shrinking so that other people won't feel insecure around you. . . . And as we let our own light shine, we unconsciously give other people permission to do the same.[1]

We can be powerful beyond measure.

Managing ourselves and leading others is a long game. As you grow as a leader and as a person, you'll encounter unexpected conditions that make leadership more difficult. Not everyone will agree with your assessment. Not everyone will be happy with your decisions. Not everyone will be on your side. Not everyone will like you. And not every decision you make will be a good one. It's these conditions that will test you and make you want to back down, to stay quiet, to give up, to stay small. And it's in these conditions when it's most important to connect with what's important to you and take the long view.

We are all in the process of becoming, and our behaviors, our choices, and our actions are our responsibility. Each new level of leadership will require an expanded set of skills. You are increasingly responsible for creating the conditions for the organization, and the people in the organization, to compete for the future. You go from focusing on your team and your projects to having to consider the short-term, mid-term, and long-term implications of your decisions and actions. And as you rise to the C-suite level, you go from a culture taker to a culture maker.

Leadership is an ambitious endeavor, and ambition is a good thing. Rarely has anything of importance been accomplished without it, including stewarding an organization and the people working there toward a more successful future. And the world needs leadership now more than ever. At this point, most of the easy problems have been solved, and we need people with the vision, ambition, and care to lead individuals, organizations, and societies toward a better future.

Being in a position of leadership is a great honor and a great commitment. You are different now than you were ten years ago. You are different now than you were five years ago. And you're different now than when you started this book. There are more S curves ahead, and that's a good thing. We get to evolve as leaders. We get to chart our course. We get to pursue big goals.

And you are ready because you've done the work. You understand the people, ideas, and situations that have shaped you as an individual and how these influences show up in your approach to leadership. You are clear on your values. You know how you define success. Your self-understanding grounds you in what's important and gives you insight into the skills and behaviors you'll need in the work to become the next version of yourself. Your self-management along a series of S curves will help you get there, as will your tool kit for addressing the many challenges in leadership and decision-making, your new understanding of what it takes to understand and lead others, your appreciation for the power of organizational culture, and your playbook for building resilience for the inevitable setbacks that accompany ambitious goals.

So play big: The world needs what you have to offer. We need your wild ideas, your creativity, your know-how, your humanity, your desire to improve the situation or organization, and your drive to make the world a better place. We need *your* leadership!

ACKNOWLEDGMENTS

It's not just raising a child that takes a village—creating a book does too. My heartfelt thanks to the village that helped me raise *this* book.

First and foremost, my gratitude goes to Chris Haley, an exemplar in understanding and managing oneself and an outstanding life partner in every sense of the word. And to Connor Haley, Alec Haley, and Erin Haley, three of my greatest teachers and sources of joy and deep pride.

To my students and program participants, it has been a pleasure to work with and learn from you over the years.

Thank you to the many people who have generously shared their stories and those who have read through various drafts of the manuscript, including Alva He, Andres Salgado-Bierman, Andy Bandyopadhyay, Ashwin Damera, Beat Buhlmann, Ben Maddahi, Camilo Delgado, Christopher Held, Connie Askin, Daniel Mouen Makoua, David Roche, Dayna Catropa, Eric Cornell, Gena Cox, Gina Azaric, Guido Meardi, Harry Robottom, Harriet Stein, Heidi Smith, Irena Asmundson, Janet Brown, Janet Ply, Jen Owings, Josh Freedman, Jules Sebastian, Kathy Oneto, Katie Doran, Lianna Kinard, Lisa Leander, Marian Poirier, Marcia Dawood, Mark Schab, Mary Rowe,

Nadine Kawkabani, Prakeerthi Jallipalli, Raj Bandyopadhyay, Rob Duboff, Rohan Rajiv, Sangeeta Saxena, Shailesh Shukla, Shaun Carver, Sue Bevan Baggott, and Tunde Fafunwa. Adrienne, Alex, Alexandra, Ashley, Carla, Charlotte, Claire, Ed, Irene, James, John, Martin, Phil, Sharon, Sofia, and Vivek were also very helpful in sharing their stories.

Thank you to Jill Marsal, who was among the first to believe in this book and provided some wonderful advice and guidance along the way, and to Emily Taber for seeing the book's potential and for her help in shaping this book and making it better in ways both large and small.

A big thanks to AJ Harper and Laura Stone for all the questions you answered, for your good humor, and for always leaving the light on for me. And to the Top Three Book Writing Group, thank you for the wonderful community and support.

APPENDIX: ADDITIONAL RESOURCES

It's difficult to narrow a list of suggested resources from the many available for learning more about the topics we cover in MYLO. Here is a relatively short list of some of my most-recommended books. If you would like to see a longer and continually updated list of additional resources, including books, articles, speeches, podcasts, videos, and films, please visit www.margaretandrews.com/mylobookresources.

Understanding Yourself

Insight: Why We're Not as Self-Aware as We Think, and How Seeing Ourselves Clearly Helps Us Succeed at Work and in Life, by Tasha Eurich (Crown Business, 2017).

Values Clarification: A Practical, Action-Directed Workbook, by Dr. Sidney B. Simon, Dr. Leland W. Howe, and Dr. Howard Kirschenbaum (Grand Central, 1995).

Emotional: How Feelings Shape Our Thinking, by Leonard Mlodinow (Vintage, 2022).

Managing Yourself

The Anxious Achiever: Turn Your Biggest Fears into Your Leadership Superpower, by Morra Aarons-Mele (Harvard Business Review Press, 2023).

Perfect Attendance: Being Present for Life, by Harriet Stein (Big Toe in the Water, 2023).

How to Break Up with Your Phone: The 30-Day Plan to Take Back Your Life, by Catherine Price (Ten Speed, 2018).

Leading Others

Difficult Conversations: How to Discuss What Matters Most, by Douglas Stone, Bruce Patton, Sheila Heen, and Roger Fisher (Penguin, 2023).

Good Team, Bad Team: Lead Your People to Go After Big Challenges, Not Each Other, by Sarah Thurber and Blair Miller (Page Two, 2024).

Getting Along: How to Work with Anyone (Even Difficult People), by Amy Gallo (Harvard Business Review Press, 2022).

Managing Up

Managing Up: How to Move Up, Win at Work, and Succeed with Any Type of Boss, by Mary Abbajay (Wiley, 2018).

Managing Your Boss, by John J. Gabarro and John P. Kotter (Harvard Business Review Press, 2008).

Influencing Up, by Allan R. Cohen and David L. Bradford (Wiley, 2012).

Understanding Organizational Culture

Organizational Culture and Leadership, 5th ed., by Edgar H. Schein (with Peter Schein) (Wiley, 2016).

The Corporate Culture Survival Guide, by Edgar H. Schein and Peter A. Schein (Wiley, 2019).

Immunity to Change: How to Overcome It and Unlock the Potential in Yourself and Your Organization, by Robert Kegan and Lisa Laskow Lahey (Harvard Business Review Press, 2009).

Unpacking the Challenges of Leadership

The Great Mental Models: General Thinking Concepts, by Shane Parrish (Portfolio, 2024).

Defining Moments: When Managers Must Choose Between Right and Right, by Joseph L. Badaracco (Harvard Business Review Press, 2016).

Both/And Thinking: Embracing Creative Tensions to Solve Your Toughest Problems, by Wendy K. Smith and Marianne W. Lewis (Harvard Business Review Press, 2022).

Resilience, Recovery, Renewal, and Reinvention

The Resilience Plan: A Strategic Approach to Optimizing Your Work Performance and Mental Health, by Marie-Helene Pelletier (Page Two, 2024).

Big Feelings: How to Be Okay When Things Are Not Okay, by Liz Fosslien and Mollie West Duffy (Portfolio, 2022).

Bittersweet: How Sorrow and Longing Make Us Whole, by Susan Cain (Crown, 2022).

NOTES

Chapter 1: Recognizing What Great Leadership Looks Like

1. Charles Riborg Mann, "A Study of Engineering Education," Carnegie Foundation for the Advancement of Teaching, Bulletin 11 (1918), 106–108.

2. Daniel Goleman, "What Makes a Leader," *Harvard Business Review*, January 2004, https://hbr.org/2004/01/what-makes-a-leader.

3. Stephen M. R. Covey, *The Speed of Trust* (Free Press, 2006), 13.

4. Linda Hill, "Becoming the Boss," *Harvard Business Review*, January 2007, https://hbr.org/2007/01/becoming-the-boss.

5. Mirjam A. Tuk, Sonja Prokopec, and Bram Van den Bergh, "Do Versus Don't: The Impact of Framing on Goal-Level Setting," *Journal of Consumer Research* 47, no. 6 (2021): 1003–1024, https://doi.org/10.1093/jcr/ucaa050.

Chapter 2: Understanding How We Grow as Leaders—and What Happens When We Don't

1. Charles Handy, *The Empty Raincoat: Making Sense of the Future* (Hutchinson, 1994), 50.

2. Marshall Goldsmith, *What Got You Here Won't Get You There* (Hyperion, 2007), 10.

3. Herminia Ibarra, "The Authenticity Paradox," *Harvard Business Review*, January–February 2015, https://hbr.org/2015/01/the-authenticity-paradox.

4. Jean Brittain Leslie and Ellen Van Velsor, "A Look at Derailment Today: North America and Europe," Center for Creative Leadership, 1996, 6–12.

5. Joyce Hogan, Robert Hogan, and Robert Kaiser, "Management Derailment: Personality Assessment and Mitigation," www.hoganassessments.com/sites/default/files/Management%20Derailment%205-1-l2009%20%282%29_0.pdf (also appears as a chapter in the *APA Handbook of Industrial and Organizational Psychology* [2010]); Michael M. Lombardo and Cynthia D. McCauley, "The Dynamics of Management Derailment," Technical Report 34, Center for Creative Leadership (July 1988), 3; Morgan W. McCall Jr. and Michael M. Lombardo, "Off the Track: Why and How Successful Executives Get Derailed," Technical Report 21, Center for Creative Leadership (1983), 7; Ellen Van Velsor and Jean Brittain Leslie, "Why

Executives Derail: Perspectives Across Time and Cultures," *Academy of Management Executive* 9, no. 4 (1995): 63–69.

6. Van Velsor and Leslie, "Why Executives Derail."

7. Lombardo and McCauley, "Dynamics of Management Derailment."

8. Hogan, Hogan, and Kaiser, "Management Derailment"; Jim Harter, "U.S. Employee Engagement Needs a Rebound in 2023," Workplace, Gallup Organization, www.gallup.com/workplace/468233/employee-engagement-needs-rebound-2023.aspx; Randall Beck and Jim Harter, "Managers Account for 70% of Variance in Employee Engagement," *Business Journal*, April 21, 2015, https://news.gallup.com/businessjournal/182792/managers-account-variance-employee-engagement.aspx.

9. Chris Westfall, "Leadership Development Is a $366 Billion Industry: Here's Why Most Programs Don't Work," *Forbes*, June 20, 2019, www.forbes.com/sites/chriswestfall/2019/06/20/leadership-development-why-most-programs-dont-work/?sh=3fdd2ce061de; "Size of the Training Industry," TrainingIndustry.com, March 29, 2021, https://trainingindustry.com/wiki/learning-services-and-outsourcing/size-of-training-industry; "Global Corporate Leadership Training Market 2022–2028 Size by Manufactures, Applications, Types, Growth, Status, and Outlook," *Absolute Reports*, March 22, 2022, www.globenewswire.com/en/news-release/2022/03/22/2407247/0/en/Global-Corporate-Leadership-Training-Market-2022-2028-Size-by-Manufactures-Applications-Types-Growth-Status-and-Outlook.html; "Preparing for the Future with Complementary Leadership," Gartner research report, 2020, www.gartner.com/en/human-resources/trends/reshaping-leadership-to-prepare-for-the-future#:~:text=To%20cultivate%20a%20strong%20leadership,and%20lead%20in%20critical%20areas.

10. Jon Clifton, "Gallup: Economic Growth Is Slowing: How Should Managers Respond?," Workplace, Gallup Organization, June 13, 2023, www.gallup.com/workplace/506825/economic-growth-slowing-leaders-respond.aspx?utm_source=workplace&utm_medium=email&utm_campaign=gallup_at_work_newsletter_send_1_june_06132023_test_a&utm_term=newsletter&utm_content=read_more_cta_1.

Chapter 3: Understanding Yourself

1. Tasha Eurich, *Insight* (Crown Business, 2017), 4.

2. David Dunning, Chip Heath, and Jerry Suls, "Flawed Self-Assessment: Implications for Health, Education, and the Workplace," *Psychological Science in the Public Interest* 5, no. 3 (2004): 69–106; Eurich, *Insight*, 4.

3. Erica Sloan, "6 Signs That a Person Lacks Self-Awareness—and Why That Could Be a Problem," WellandGood.com, February 21, 2023, www.wellandgood.com/lifestyle/signs-low-self-awareness; Travis Bradberry, *Emotional Intelligence Habits: Change Your Habits, Change Your Life* (TalentSmartEQ, 2023),

16–18; Kendra Cherry, "Signs of Low Emotional Intelligence," VeryWellMind .com, July 12, 2020, www.verywellmind.com/signs-of-low-emotional-intelligence -2795958; Robert Hogan and Rodney Warrenfeltz, "Educating the Modern Manager," *Academy of Learning and Education* 2, no. 1 (2003): 74–84.

4. "Detecting Derailers: Recognizing the Warning Signs Before High-Potential Leaders or New Hires Go Off Track," Korn Ferry Institute, 2014, www.kornferry.com /content/dam/kornferry/docs/article-migration/Korn-Ferry_Institute_Detecting -derailers.pdf.

Chapter 4: Managing Yourself

1. Jennifer Porter, "How to Move from Self-Awareness to Self-Improvement," *Harvard Business Review*, June 19, 2019, https://hbr.org/2019/06/how-to-move -from-self-awareness-to-self-improvement.

2. "What Are Emotions?," Paul Ekman Group, www.paulekman.com/universal -emotions/#:~:text=In%20other%20words%2C%20emotions%20prepare,just %20happen%20to%20us%20automatically; Kendra Cherry, "Emotions and Types of Emotional Responses," Very Well Mind, June 29, 2023, www.verywellmind.com /what-are-emotions-2795178.

3. The Atlas of Emotion, https://atlasofemotions.org/#continents; Heather C. Lench, ed., *The Function of Emotions: When and Why Emotions Help Us* (Springer, 2018); "What Are Emotions?"

4. Susan David, "The Gift and Power of Emotional Courage," TED Talk, TEDWomen, November 2017, www.ted.com/talks/susan_david_the_gift_and_power _of_emotional_courage.

5. Tasha Eurich, "What Self-Awareness Really Is (and How to Cultivate It)," *Harvard Business Review*, January 4, 2018, https://hbr.org/2018/01/what-self -awareness-really-is-and-how-to-cultivate-it; Tasha Eurich, "Working with People Who Aren't Self-Aware," *Harvard Business Review*, October 19, 2018, https://hbr .org/2018/10/working-with-people-who-arent-self-aware.

6. Steven Stosny, "Self-Regulation," *Psychology Today*, October 28, 2011, www.psychologytoday.com/us/blog/anger-in-the-age-entitlement/201110/self -regulation.

7. "William James," Goodreads, www.goodreads.com/quotes/108925-actions -seems-to-follow-feeling-but-really-actions-and-feeling.

8. Amal Ahmadi and Bernd Vogel, "Knowing but Not Enacting Leadership: Navigating the Leadership Knowing-Doing Gap in Leveraging Leadership Development," *Academy of Management Learning & Education* 22, no. 3 (2023): 507–530, https://doi.org/10.5465/amle.2020.0534.

9. Todd Herman, *The Alter Ego Effect: The Power of Secret Identities to Transform Your Life* (HarperCollins, 2019), 33.

Chapter 5: Leading Others

1. Ed Catmull, *Creativity, Inc.* (Random House, 2023), xiv.

2. Timothy A. Judge, Ronald F. Piccolo, Nathan P. Podsakoff, John C. Shaw, and Bruce L. Rich, "The Relationship Between Pay and Job Satisfaction: A Meta-Analysis of the Literature," *Journal of Vocational Behavior* 77 (2010): 157–167.

3. Tomas Chamorro-Premuzic, "Does Money Really Affect Motivation? A Review of the Research," *Harvard Business Review*, April 10, 2013, https://hbr.org/2013/04/does-money-really-affect-motiv.

4. Lou Soloman, "Becoming Powerful Makes You Less Empathetic," *Harvard Business Review*, April 21, 2015, https://hbr.org/2015/04/becoming-powerful-makes-you-less-empathetic.

5. Quoted in Yasmin Anwar, "Why Does Power Make Us Lose Our Way?," *University of California News*, May 17, 2016, www.universityofcalifornia.edu/news/why-does-power-make-us-lose-our-way.

6. Mark Goulston and John Ullmen, *Real Influence: Persuade Without Pushing and Gain Without Giving In* (AMACOM, 2013), 93–106.

7. Stephanie Neal, Rosey Rhyne, Jazmine Boatman, Bruce Watt, and Mindy Yeh, "Global Leadership Forecast 2023," 10, www.ddiworld.com/global-leadership-forecast-2023.

8. Andrew Molinsky and Joshua Margolis, "Necessary Evils and Interpersonal Sensitivity in Organizations," *Academy of Management Review* 30, no. 2 (2005): 245–268.

9. Martha Legace, "Conducting Layoffs: 'Necessary Evils' at Work," *Harvard Business School Working Knowledge*, July 6, 2009, www.library.hbs.edu/working-knowledge/conducting-layoffs-necessary-evils-at-work.

Chapter 6: Managing Up

1. Joyce Hogan, Robert Hogan, and Robert Kaiser, "Management Derailment: Personality Assessment and Mitigation," www.hoganassessments.com/sites/default/files/Management%20Derailment%205-1-l2009%20%282%29_0.pdf.

2. Lindsey Leake, "Senior Leaders Are Up to 12× More Likely to Be Psychopaths—How to Spot an Abusive Boss," *Fortune*, July 12, 2024, https://fortune.com/well/article/workplace-abuse-toxic-boss-psychopath; Harris Poll, "Toxic Bosses Survey: What They Do & How We Cope," October 2023, https://theharrispoll.com/wp-content/uploads/2023/10/Toxic-Bosses-Survey-October-2023.pdf.

3. Christine Porath and Christine Pearson, "The Price of Incivility," *Harvard Business Review*, January–February 2013, https://hbr.org/2013/01/the-price-of-incivility.

4. "Thich Nhat Hanh," Goodreads, www.goodreads.com/quotes/4310-when-another-person-makes-you-suffer-it-is-because-he.

5. "Dave Willis," Goodreads, www.goodreads.com/quotes/7419009-show-respect-to-people-who-don-t-even-deserve-it-not.

Chapter 7: Understanding Organizational Culture

1. Boris Groysberg, Jeremiah Lee, Jesse Price, and J. Yo-Jud Cheng, "The Leader's Guide to Corporate Culture," *Harvard Business Review*, January–February 2018, https://store.hbr.org/product/the-leader-s-guide-to-corporate-culture/S18010?sku=S18010-PDF-ENG.

2. Edgar H. Schein and Peter A. Schein, *Organizational Culture and Leadership*, 5th ed. (Wiley, 2017), 17–25.

3. Schein and Schein, *Organizational Culture and Leadership*, 25.

4. Quoted in Lindsey Leake, "Senior Leaders Are Up to 12× More Likely to Be Psychopaths—How to Spot an Abusive Boss," *Fortune*, July 12, 2024, https://fortune.com/well/article/workplace-abuse-toxic-boss-psychopath.

5. Schein and Schein, *Organizational Culture and Leadership*, 131.

6. Donald Sull and Charles Sull, "10 Things Your Corporate Culture Needs to Get Right," *MIT Sloan Management Review*, September 16, 2021, https://sloanreview.mit.edu/article/10-things-your-corporate-culture-needs-to-get-right.

7. Stanley Holmes, "Gates Admits Grim Defeat, Urges Staff to Maintain Focus," *Los Angeles Times*, June 9, 2000, www.latimes.com/archives/la-xpm-2000-jun-09-fi-39117-story.html.

8. Kurt Eichenwald, "Microsoft's Lost Decade," *Vanity Fair*, July 24, 2012, https://archive.vanityfair.com/article/2012/8/microsofts-lost-decade.

9. Steve Balmer to Microsoft Employees, July 11, 2013, One Microsoft, https://news.microsoft.com/2013/07/11/one-microsoft-company-realigns-to-enable-innovation-at-greater-speed-efficiency-2.

10. Satya Nadella, *Hit Refresh* (HarperCollins, 2017).

11. Satya Nadella to Microsoft Employees, February 4, 2014, RE: Satya Nadella—Microsoft's New CEO, https://news.microsoft.com/2014/02/04/satya-nadella-email-to-employees-on-first-day-as-ceo.

12. Boris Groysberg, Jeremiah Lee, Jesse Price, and J. Yo-Jud Cheng, "The Leader's Guide to Corporate Culture," *Harvard Business Review*, January–February 2018, 9–10.

Chapter 8: Unpacking the Challenges of Leadership

1. Sally Raskoff, "Interpreting Research Results: Probabilities, Not Certainties," *Everyday Sociology Blog*, May 1, 2014, www.everydaysociologyblog.com/2014/05/interpreting-research-results-probabilities-not-certainties.html.

2. "Coffee," Nutrition Source, https://nutritionsource.hsph.harvard.edu/food-features/coffee/.

3. Karen Sternheimer, "Why Social Science Research Matters," *Everyday Sociology Blog*, July 1, 2019, www.everydaysociologyblog.com/2019/07/why-social-science-research-matters.html.

4. Teresa M. Amabile, "How to Kill Creativity," *Harvard Business Review*, September–October 1998, https://hbr.org/1998/09/how-to-kill-creativity.

Chapter 9: Recovering from Setbacks, Getting Unstuck, and Building Resilience

1. Steve Jobs, "'You've Got to Find What You Love,' Jobs Says," 2005 Stanford University commencement address, *Stanford Report*, June 12, 2005, https://news.stanford.edu/stories/2005/06/youve-got-find-love-jobs-says.

2. Andrea Ovans, "What Resilience Means, and Why It Matters," *Harvard Business Review*, January 5, 2015, https://hbr.org/2015/01/what-resilience-means-and-why-it-matters.

3. "Building Your Resilience," American Psychological Association, January 1, 2012, www.apa.org/topics/resilience/building-your-resilience.

4. Gina Kolata, "Long Overlooked, Kati Kariko Helped Shield the World from the Coronavirus," *New York Times*, April 8, 2021, updated April 17, 2021, www.nytimes.com/2021/04/08/health/coronavirus-mrna-kariko.html; Benjamin Mueller and Gina Kolata, "Nobel Prize Awarded to COVID Vaccine Pioneers," *New York Times*, October 2, 2023, updated October 3, 2023, www.nytimes.com/2023/10/02/health/nobel-prize-medicine.html.

Chapter 10: The Long View

1. Marianne Williamson, *A Return to Love* (HarperCollins, 1992), 190–191.

INDEX

Credit: Raj Bandyopadhyay Series A Photography

Margaret C. Andrews is a seasoned executive, academic leader, speaker, and instructor. She has created and teaches a variety of leadership courses and professional and executive programs at Harvard University and is the founder of the MYLO Center, a private leadership development firm. Her clients include Amazon, Citi, Continental, the United Nations, Walmart, and Wayfair. She lives in Brookline, Massachusetts.